THE SOUND OF HIS VOICE

THE SOUND OF HIS VOICE

KIM CLEMENT

CREATION
HOUSE
BOOKS ABOUT SPIRIT-LED LIVING
ORLANDO, FLORIDA

Creation House
Strang Communications Company
600 Rinehart Road
Lake Mary, FL 32746

First printing, November 1993
Second printing, January 1994
Third printing, May 1994
Fourth printing, June 1994

To my wife, Jane,
my daughters, Donné and Jacquelyn,
and my son, Caleb,
for their love and encouragement

ACKNOWLEDGMENTS

- God

- Gloria Barnes, my mother-in-law, for her tireless hours of editing.

- Fred and Nellie Roberts, for their spiritual input and covering over the years.

- Peter and Leslie Frederic, for introducing me to Jesus and for their patience while discipling me.

- Neil Eskelin, for all his help in putting these ideas on paper.

- And my staff — Debbie, Allan and Theresa — for their assistance.

IN THIS book I often give examples from my personal life to illustrate the teaching. I do this with great hesitancy and concern because I do not want to seem as if I am boasting of myself. As Paul says, "God forbid that I should boast except in the cross of our Lord Jesus Christ" (Gal. 6:14). So please accept these anecdotes as teaching tools and not as my trying to glorify myself.

ONE

A Shattered Dream

I'M ONLY seventeen, and I'm dying, I thought as I pressed my hand against my chest, trying in vain to stop the blood that was flowing from a deep stab wound near my shoulder.

I staggered to the bathroom of that rock club in Port Elizabeth, South Africa, and everything around me became a giant blur. My mind was so drugged with alcohol and dope that I didn't even know who had stabbed me — or why.

"Isn't anyone going to help me?" I cried as I stuffed paper towels inside my shirt to fight the hemorrhaging. But no one heard me. I was alone.

I lurched out of the bathroom, struggled through the crowded club and fell on my face in the gutter outside. *Everybody here knows me,* I thought, *but nobody cares.*

As a musician I had headlined in that club countless times. My name had been plastered in the papers because of a movie contract I had just signed with an Australian film company. Even that very night the people were congratulating me. "Let's hear it for Kim!" they cheered. "Way to go!"

No one knew it, but my life had actually reached a point of hopelessness and despair. Everything I tried seemed so exciting at the start, but with each success came an emptiness in the pit of my stomach that I could not explain. Twice that same month I had tried to take my own life. Now it seemed as if someone had done it for me.

Is this how it is going to end? I thought. *Is my life over?*

Cracking My Knuckles

In 1956, I was born in Uitenhage, South Africa. The place was called Uitenhage, a town of about fifty thousand people on the outskirts of the city of Port Elizabeth. It is a coastal area about halfway between Cape Town and Durban.

My father, Vivian, had a government job with the housing department of the railways, and my mother, Babette, worked at odd jobs to help make a living for the family. I was the second of four children — three boys and a girl. We lived in a modest, but comfortable, brick home at 10 Butler Street. It was on a hill that overlooked the Uitenhage railroad station.

Like most white South African families, we had a black maid who came to work every day from the segregated township where she lived. Her name was Hilda and, even though she was African, she was like a second mother to me.

As far back as I can remember, my parents told me, "Kim, you are going to be a classical pianist." In fact, they insisted that all of us — my two brothers, my sister and I — be trained in music.

When I was five I started piano lessons with my Aunt Belle. It was a painful experience. She was a demanding teacher and would crack my knuckles with a pencil if I made a mistake. But before long I played "After the Ball" at a recital. Then my mother enrolled me in classical music at the local branch of Trinity College of London. It was a rigorous program that included an annual musical examination.

Every day I would practice two or three hours on our old upright piano, and by the time I was nine or ten, my motivation was no longer external. I *wanted* to practice. I craved to perform. And I began to believe that I was destined to be an outstanding musician. I dreamed about performing great concerts and traveling the world.

Once my mother took me to a fortune-teller who told me, "Young man, I see that you will one day go overseas as a musician and become famous."

Going to a clairvoyant was nothing unusual in our home. We were a Christian family only in the broadest sense of the term. I certainly did not have a God-fearing upbringing. The only time we visited the local Methodist church was to meet some friends or to attend a wedding or a funeral.

Yes, we believed there was a God. Yes, we celebrated Christmas. But we were never encouraged to read the Bible or to know the side of Christianity that emphasized a relationship with Jesus Christ. We barely even knew the religious side.

To say that we were a liberal family is an understatement. By the time I was nine I was smoking, and my parents never stopped me. It's not that my mother and father were evil or immoral people — they just wanted their children to be "free" and expressive.

I can still remember what happened after I had an unfortunate accident in our home when I was about ten years old. While my parents were working, my brother and I were playing, and I fell out of a cupboard that was quite high. When I hit the floor, I stopped breathing and was rushed to the hospital. The damage to one of my hips was so severe that I was under medical care for nearly three months.

One day an Anglican minister, wearing his clerical collar, came into my hospital room. He walked over to my bed and asked, "Would you like me to pray with you?"

"No," I instinctively responded, "I don't want any prayer." Then he looked me straight in the eye and said something that sounded quite unusual to me, "Jesus still walks the streets today, and one day you are going to need Him. If you call on Him, He'll walk over to you, and He will touch you."

I didn't respond to his words, and he quietly left the room.

Forbidden Friends

When I was eleven I told my mother, "I'm through with classical music. You can forget about any more lessons." I had discovered other styles of music — and I was drawn in.

Jazz was just a brief fling before rock and roll became the new force that dominated every waking moment of my life. I listened to it on the radio, bought cassette tapes and began to play it on my electronic keyboard. My new desire was to become a rock star.

Every time I looked at the train station that was down the hill from our house, I dreamed about getting on one of those trains and going to wherever the tracks would lead.

I used to go to Port Elizabeth to hear almost every rock group that came into town. I didn't have to sneak out of the house. That wasn't necessary. My parents let me do my own thing.

That same year I began playing in my first rock band. We were called Mark IV.

Growing up in South Africa in the 1960s and 1970s, I was surrounded by conflict and strife. In every direction there was hate and mistrust.

Many of our neighbors were shocked that some of my best friends were blacks — all of them musicians. The controversy grew when I performed with a "colored" rock group named The Invaders. I thought nothing about venturing into black townships where whites were forbidden because my friends lived there.

Most of the world sees the problem of South Africa as a political struggle between blacks and whites. But the roots of the hostility run much deeper. In reality the clash includes black against black and white against white.

In my own home, for example, great hatred existed toward Afrikaners — white people of Dutch descent. My parents had British origins — my dad was Scottish and my mother was from an English family which had lived in South Africa for generations. We learned to speak Afrikaans, the "kitchen Dutch" language that was spoken in our community. But we detested it. At home we spoke only English.

Whites make up only about 18 percent of the population, but they are divided into two distinct camps. Three-fifths are Afrikaners, and the remaining are English. Their strife stems from the war fought at the turn of the century between the Boers, or Dutch farmers, and the Uitlanders, or "foreigners" (who were mainly British). Each had settled huge geographical areas of the territory. The stakes were high. The world's largest gold and diamond mines had been discovered, and a bitter struggle for power ensued. Even though the forces of Great Britain prevailed, and the Union of South Africa was established in 1910, the hatred and mistrust continues to this day.

A conflict also exists between the blacks and the "coloreds," the part-white descendants of several African peoples who mingled with the first white settlers. They are the most rejected people in the country and are despised by tribal blacks.

Asians, mainly from India, make up only 3 percent of the

13

population, but they also live in a constant state of turmoil. The blacks hate the Asians; the Hindus hate the Muslims. And the Indian Christians are the target of even more antagonism.

South Africa is the only major nation in the world where a racial minority controls the government. In 1948 *apartheid* became the official law of the land. It is an Afrikaans word meaning "apartness." Its aim was to keep the four main racial groups (whites, blacks, coloreds and Asians) strictly separated — socially and politically.

Apartheid laws have affected every aspect of life in South Africa. Although 73 percent of the population is black, they have been severely restricted regarding where they can live, where they can work and the education they can receive. Even the church has become an extension of apartheid. From pulpits across the land white ministers have preached that the Bible endorses separation of the races.

The historic riots in the native housing areas of Soweto and Sharpsville were, in large part, ignited by the attempt to force the black population to learn the Afrikaans language.

In America, racial segregation was symbolized by signs on the seats of public buses that read, "Blacks only beyond this point." In South Africa the entire bus was segregated. Signs on drinking fountains and rest rooms said, "Whites only" — and often no facilities existed at all for blacks.

The response from the world community has been one of moral outrage. Economic sanctions and sports boycotts have attempted to isolate the country politically. But inside the country, although social apartheid laws have been officially abolished, the cauldron continues to boil. People wonder if democracy will prevail. Will the rule of the white minority end without a bloodbath?

An Incorrigible Truant

At the age of thirteen I didn't care about such weighty matters as African nationalism or racial politics. I was a young rebel, and I couldn't care less what others thought. I regularly used marijuana and bragged about it. Every few months my friends and I would form a new music group. One of them, the Purple Fez, was punk rock, so we all dressed in outlandish purple outfits.

At the heart of everything we did was a rebellion against authority. I was always the youngest member of the group, running with a fast crowd in their late teens and early twenties.

Our great idols were the Beatles, Jimi Hendrix, Janis Joplin and Deep Purple. We would not only listen to their tapes, but we'd try to dress like them, copy their stage movements — even take the same drugs.

My older brother Barry played the trumpet, and he joined our rock group at the dances and "sessions" we played. We began to get bookings everywhere — from golf clubs and pubs to colleges. Soon we were playing venues in Port Elizabeth, East London and Cape Town. Then came The Cosmic Blues. It was the show band — an eighteen-piece rock group that played to audiences that numbered in the thousands. I was on the keyboard/synthesizer and did some of the vocals.

What about my education? I was expelled from three different schools because I was so unruly. Somehow I felt like a misfit who didn't belong. I was in a society where the blacks were rejected, yet they were my friends. The English white people were rejected, yet they were my family.

It wasn't only school that I hated. Except for my music, I hated everything about the first seventeen years of my life. Educational authorities labeled me as an incorrigible truant because I would stay away from school for weeks at a time.

Above our house were two hills. At the top of one of them was a public park and a sizable monument in honor of King George V, the monarch who was on the throne when the Union of South Africa was formed. Standing at the base of the monument provides a great view of the entire city of Uitenhage.

Once, for a period of about three weeks, I climbed that hill every morning and just sat there, desperately unhappy. I waited for my parents to leave for work, and then I would go back to the house, take my drugs and listen to my collection of rock music. The school authorities finally picked me up, and the principal gave me "six of the best" — with a cane.

The problem became even more serious when the officials found drugs on me — I was expelled. My parents could not find any school in our town that would admit me. They finally took me to Port Elizabeth and enrolled me in the Lawson Brown School. The headmaster, after hearing my story and calling the principal in Uitenhage, said, "Look, I know you have a problem, but we are going to take a chance on you." Then he added, "As a Christian, I feel that is the least I can do."

It was obvious that my rebellious streak was like a wild horse that would not be tamed. The drug use and pattern of truancy continued until I was eventually asked to leave. Before my seventeenth birthday I was a druggie who had turned to the "hard stuff." I became addicted to heroin, and my life seemed to be vanishing before me.

South Africa is very strict about drug use, but I knew where to obtain drugs and still stay out of trouble with the authorities. No cocaine was available at that time, but I had a source for heroin. And with the money I was making in music, I was able to afford it.

In the Finals

I remember the day my mother came to me and said, "Kim, there is something I want you to do."

"Go ahead. Tell me what it is," I responded.

She showed me the promotional brochure for an international music competition being held in Port Elizabeth. "I believe you can win the best keyboard artist category, and then you would represent South Africa in the finals in Japan." The event was sponsored by Yamaha.

It was obvious why Mom wanted me to enter the contest. It was her chance to show her friends that all my early music training had not been wasted and that I was a serious musician after all. So I told her, "If it will make you happy, I'll do it."

The contest turned out to be a major event. I succeeded in the preliminary rounds and was in the spotlight in the finals that were held at the city hall. The format of the competition was unique, to say the least. Each contestant performed for about eight minutes until he or she was stopped by a loud bell.

That night, however, I was so drugged and drunk when I was playing that I never did hear that bell. I just kept going until they stopped me. Of course, the judges realized that I was on some kind of pills — and my dress code left much to be desired. They awarded me second place. My bruised ego, however, was consoled by two newspaper critics and a magazine columnist who wrote that I should have won it all.

I lost. But in the audience was a film producer from Australia who had flown in to shoot some footage along the South African coast. His crew was filming a movie called *A Winter's Tale*. To my surprise, the producer approached me with a proposal. "We'd really like you to do some original music for this movie," he said.

"Great!" I was enthusiastic.

Immediately I began to immerse myself in the project. I felt as if it was going to be my big break. The newspapers wrote about how this young man from Uitenhage was hired to score the music for a motion picture. It was an important event for our family.

Financially, the contract was generous. I was scheduled to travel to Australia for the film's premier. "You don't know how lucky you are," my friends told me.

But once again I felt absolutely empty and miserable. I would practice for several hours and then turn to drugs and alcohol. I felt as if my life was spinning out of control. It was a cycle I could not seem to break.

Two events should have shaken me to my core.

One evening I came to my house and had a seizure — obviously from a bad combination of drugs. All I remember was grabbing a knife with a long blade from the kitchen. Then I blanked out. When I gained my senses, I realized I was stabbing myself repeatedly in my stomach. Blood was everywhere. It was as if I was trying to kill myself without my consciousness knowing it.

A few weeks later that same feeling came over me. I didn't know anything about Satan at the time, but I sensed that an evil power was attempting to possess my life. Perhaps the devil knew that something unusual was about to happen, and he wanted to torment me — even kill me.

Another time I was listening to a recording of *Jesus Christ Superstar*. I played it again and again even though it made me miserable. The more I heard it, the more agitated I became. *Who is this Jesus?* I asked myself. *And why are these people singing about Him?*

While the record was playing, I again felt that my actions were being controlled by a great, diabolical power. I blacked out. And when I came around, I was horrified to realize that I had taken the mouthpiece from my brother's trumpet and was stabbing at my eye and my forehead with the small part of it. The blood was flowing down my cheek and onto my shirt. There were small cuts and wounds all over my head. Something was going terribly wrong.

It was obvious that I was desperate to have something dramatically change the course of my life.

"Is It Over?"

One evening I stopped working on the film project and decided to hang out at one of the Port Elizabeth rock clubs where I had been performing. The depression that had come over me was especially powerful that night. When I got to the club I took some heroin and began to drink anything strong enough to numb my mind.

That's when it happened. For no earthly reason, someone walked up and stabbed me in the chest in that noisy, crowded club. I staggered to the bathroom and tried to stop the bleeding. Then in confusion I pushed my way out into the street.

Is this how it is going to end? I wondered. *Is my life over?*

Suddenly the words of that Anglican minister arose from deep within my spirit. I was only nine when he visited me in my hospital room, but I could still hear the sound of his voice. "Jesus still walks the streets today, and one day you are going to need Him. If you call on Him, He'll walk over to you, and He will touch you." Those words to me had been prophetic — though it would be several years before I even understood what the word *prophetic* meant.

Now, lying helpless in a gutter, I said to myself, *The only hope I have is Jesus.* I was bleeding very badly and in my despair, I said, "Jesus, if You are still walking the streets, come over to me now." And He did.

At that precise moment a man walked by who knew Jesus. This young man in his late twenties became the hands of God extended and the voice of God to me. He was a total stranger, but he picked me up off the ground, carried me to his car and drove me to the hospital.

They stitched me up, but I don't remember anything that happened during those next three days. When I "came to," the compassionate stranger was sitting in the room, waiting for me. I was released from the hospital, and he drove me to our home in Uitenhage.

When we arrived at the house, I was still in terrible pain and wanted to take more drugs. I was having withdrawal symptoms because of the three days of going cold turkey at the hospital.

It was then that he said to me, "I want to tell you about my best friend. His name is Jesus."

For the next few hours he revealed God's wonderful plan of salvation to me. Never before had I heard a story like that. I didn't argue with him or question his claims. Instead I drank in every word like a thirsty child. He didn't say, "Kim, you need to come to church and get saved." He spoke the words, "Jesus is here right now. He wants to touch you."

"What do I need to do to know Jesus?" I asked.

He led me in the sinner's prayer, and I gave my heart to the Lord. Without question it was the most incredible thing that had ever happened to me. The weight of a lifetime was immediately lifted from me.

I wish I could tell you that this man became my lifelong friend and led me in the ways of the Lord. But that is not what happened. Instead, he was like an angel of mercy who visited my life and was gone. He didn't even return to follow up on his new convert.

A friend of mine, Manie Human, did tell me where I should go to church. "You need to come with me to the Full Gospel Church of God. That's the only place you should go."

Since he seemed so sure about it, I asked, "What kind of church is that?"

"Oh, they clap their hands and sing with excitement over there," he said.

As a rock musician that enticed me. But I wanted to know more. "Is it an English church?"

"No," he said, "it's Afrikaans."

You must understand that all my life I had been opposed to attending church. But an Afrikaans church? That would have been totally out of the question. But not now. I couldn't wait to get there.

Wild and Teased

The next Sunday morning, in December 1973, I put on the only suit I owned — it was a pitch-black one. Then I found my way to the church he told me about, which was only one mile from my house.

From the moment I walked into the building, people began to turn their heads and look at me. I suppose I did look a little out of place. I was extremely thin. My hair was very long — down to my shoulders. And it was wild and teased. I stood out in that ultraconservative church where the women wore their hair in buns and didn't wear jewelry or makeup.

But they seemed to tolerate me.

The church seated about four hundred, but there were at best seventy-five people in attendance. The congregation was mainly older folks with just a few young people. The minister was known as Pastor Pretorius. He reminded me of an old wrestler — a big fellow with a round face and a broken nose.

The praise and worship were wonderful. They were clapping their hands and singing music I had never heard before. I did my best to follow along. Then, during the first part of the meeting, Pastor Pretorius stopped the music and said, "I feel led to change the order of this service. If anyone is here who needs to make a public confession of his sins before God, I want you to come down to the altar. We want to pray with you."

Without hesitation I walked forward and knelt at the altar. Several people gathered around me for a time of prayer, and afterward I went back to my seat. I learned later that the pastor had never before given an altar call during the early part of a service. Perhaps it was just for me.

When the meeting was over, a man in his twenties came over to meet me. "Hello. My name is Peter Frederic, and this is my wife, Leslie."

They were a friendly couple. Peter said, "I think I know where you are coming from, and I want to help you. You've been on drugs, haven't you?"

"You're right."

"Well, I can see your withdrawal symptoms," he said. "I know what is happening."

It had been only a few days since I had been off drugs, but he could see the telltale signs by the way I walked and talked.

"Can you come over to our house for lunch?" he asked.

"I'd love to."

Peter was a Mauritian, a Creole-speaking Frenchman from the island of Mauritius — about five hundred miles east of Madagascar in the Indian Ocean. He had been a big drug pusher who smuggled illegal substances from his homeland to Durban.

No one else in that church could have handled so ably the complex problem I was going through at that time. The others didn't know anything about druggies or *muzos*, which is the local term for musicians.

It was during one of his trips to Durban that Peter had been wonderfully saved. He and his wife then came to visit his sister who lived in Uitenhage and decided to start a business there. That was only a month before I gave my heart to the Lord. I believe the Lord brought Peter to my town because He knew I would need such a person.

Seated in his living room, Peter began to pray over me for deliverance because he knew what kinds of things I had been through. The suffering I had experienced was dreadful. The pain was deeper than people will ever know.

Peter Frederic placed a high priority on the power of confession. All that afternoon he kept asking, "What have you done in your life that you need forgiveness for? Go ahead and speak it out."

When I would name something, he would immediately pray that it would be removed forever. Then he'd inquire, "What is it that you are hiding? Try to remember it and vocalize it. You've got to empty yourself of it." Then we would pray again.

Never had I been so open and honest with anyone else in my life. But instead of feeling shame for what I had done, I felt as if my life was being totally cleansed.

"I believe you are ready to be filled with the Holy Spirit," he said at last.

"What is that?" I wanted to know.

He did his best to tell me what happened on the day of Pentecost and how it is still happening today. Then he said, "Oh, it's too hard to explain. But you'll understand when you receive Him."

We began to pray out loud, and suddenly something like a tidal wave of God's glory hit me. There in his home I was filled with the Holy Spirit and began shouting and rejoicing. I spoke in an unknown tongue for several hours. It was as if I was being immersed in fire and rain at the same time. Even the tips of my fingers and toes were tingling with a power I had never felt before.

"You've Gone Crazy!"

Later that night I came bouncing into my house like someone from another planet. I was so filled with the Spirit that I was still screaming and shouting for joy. My parents were both home, and I could see the looks of absolute horror on their faces.

"Let me tell you what has happened to me," I said. "I've met Jesus. And I've been filled with the Holy Spirit."

They just stared at me.

"No more music, no more rock bands, no more movies," I told them. "I'm giving the whole lot up. It is finished."

It was as if there had been a death in the family.

"You're off your head. You've gone crazy" was their response. My mother specifically was very angry with me because I was giving up my music career. She placed a higher priority on social lifestyle than on religion. Up to that point, my music had been one of the major bragging points in her life.

No one in my family had ever had such a religious experience. I was the first person in an entire generation who had found salvation through Christ.

For the next several months a total breakdown in communication occurred between my parents and me. Even though I continued to live at home, they did not want to discuss my religious experience. They treated me like a stranger.

But my salvation was real. The good money I had been making in music now seemed meaningless. That week I wrote letters to my rock band and to the movie producer to tell them I was finished with that part of my life.

However, I couldn't seem to esape the contract with the band. I went to my new friend, Peter, and said, "I can't play rock music anymore — not even one more show."

When I called the band manager, he said, "There is no escape clause. You'll either fulfill this contract, or I will have to take you to court."

That difficult situation provided the opportunity for me to pray one of my first prayers as a new Christian. "Lord, please help me to be released from this contract. I don't want to go back into that life."

On Friday night I was supposed to be at the club. But something amazing happened. That Friday afternoon I received a call saying that several other members of the band had been rushed to the hospital with food poisoning. The gig was canceled along with the contract! That was my final weekend in the rock music business.

I Heard a Voice

With the pressure at home, I couldn't wait for Sunday morning to come so I could return to the Full Gospel Church of God. I walked through the door with a big smile on my face; I wasn't prepared for the reception I was about to receive. I was greeted by a burly deacon who had a deep scowl on his face. Instead of giving me a warm handshake, he grabbed me by the arm and literally threw me out of the building. "We don't want your kind back here at all," he shouted.

I began to walk away, confused and angry. But my friend Peter saw what was happening and came running after me. "Don't worry about him," he said. "It's just that the way you dress and the way you wear your hair is too radical for him. He can't handle it."

"I'm not sure I belong here," I said with great disappointment.

"Don't give up now," Peter said. "Just go and cut your hair."

I managed a little smile and said, "Peter, you are talking about something very sacred now. I can make a lot of changes, but don't ask me to cut my hair."

"No, Kim." Peter disagreed. "If you want to learn about Jesus in this church, you need to cut your hair. There is no use offending these people."

"Peter," I argued, "you are asking me to give up my life. It has taken me *years* to grow my hair this long."

The next day I went to my sister-in-law Vanessa and said,

"Start cutting! I want it really short." And that's what she did. When I returned to the church next Sunday, the people at the door said, "Welcome. Is this your first visit?" They didn't even recognize me.

After a few weeks the pastor came to me and said, "Kim, you need to be baptized in water. That's what the Bible says you should do after being saved."

The baptismal service was on January 1, 1974, and it seems like only yesterday. What a service! The word had spread among my rock 'n' roll friends that something had happened to me. "He's flipped. We've got to go and check it out." At every church meeting more and more of my old pals showed up. The night of my baptism more than 150 young people came from all over the region. Motorcycles lined the street, and people in the neighborhood were bewildered.

The visitors looked rather scruffy. The deacon who had once thrown me out was overwhelmed, so he tried to keep them out. I had to plead for their cause. "How are we ever going to see these people saved? We've got to let them in!"

The deacons decided to separate my friends from the rest of the congregation and let them all sit in the balcony. It was like a spiritual apartheid, but it was better than nothing.

When the time came for me to be baptized, Pastor Pretorius prayed over me and said, "In the name of the Father, the Son and the Holy Ghost," and he put me under the water. I was immersed from my feet to the top of my short hair. The moment I came out of the water I heard a voice that I had never heard before. It was speaking to me as clearly as anything I had ever heard. It was God's voice.

How did I know it was the Lord speaking? Friend, when God speaks, you won't have to wonder. You'll just know.

The Lord said two distinct things to me. First He said, "I am calling you to be a minister of the gospel."

The minute I heard those words, I shouted out from the

26

baptismal tank, "God's called me! God's called me to the ministry!"

I'm sure the preacher felt like putting me back under the water.

Then God spoke again and gave me an incredible prophetic word. He said, "None of your household will go to the grave without salvation."

That night, many of my friends found Christ as their Savior. But what about my mother and father? What about my brothers and sister? Had I really heard from God?

TWO

WAITING IN
THE HALLWAY

"I KNOW you think you've been called to preach, but I don't believe it," said Pastor Pretorius. I had only been a Christian for a few weeks, and he was already giving me a stern lecture.

"Here's what we want you to do," he said forcefully. "We want you to sit in this church for at least three years — no music ministry, no preaching, no nothing!"

Then he got to the core of the matter. "If you are prepared to be faithful to this church and hear what God has to say, we will build your character and drive this rebellion out of you."

Things were happening so fast in my life that I hardly knew how to respond. In just over a month I had been stabbed, saved, sent to church, filled with the Spirit, rejected by my family, freed from drugs, kicked out of church, baptized in water and spoken to by God. Now I was being grounded.

"Pastor," I said, "you know what is best for my life. God brought me here for a purpose, and I am ready to learn."

That church provided exactly what I needed most: discipline. Most pastors would have brought me to the platform and let me use my talent for the Lord. But not here. They believed I needed to sit in the pew and become a student of the Word. The church was legalistic, dogmatic and uncompromising, but for me it was the greatest thing that could have ever happened.

Pastor Pretorius was an important influence in my life, but Peter Frederic was the one who discipled me and became my spiritual father. I shudder to think what my life would have become without his influence.

Peter and I would pray together for hours and hours — walking up and down the aisles of the church, praying in the Spirit. More than once we entered into forty days of fasting and prayer.

To earn a little money, I took a job as a storeman in the parts department at a Volkswagen factory. I was fortunate to have any job at all since I was a high school dropout and had no skills other than music.

During my first year as a Christian, there were only three major activities in my life: working, praying and studying God's Word. Every time the doors of the church were open, I was there. Peter and I continued our daily prayer meetings, and my understanding of God's Spirit grew like a tree planted in good soil.

Gone "Bonkers"

At home the tension grew worse. At first my parents would not speak to me about my experience with Jesus. Even when we would talk, we had nothing in common. I had become one of those "strict" Christians. I wouldn't go to the movies. I wouldn't listen to rock music. I only wanted to be in the presence of the Lord — and my parents didn't.

One night a hypnotist came to our town to put on a show. My parents said, "Kim, come see the show with us."

"No," I told them. "That is not of the Lord."

They couldn't understand.

The pastor would not allow me to play the piano publicly, but I felt a tremendous need to release the music that was inside me. Every chance I had I came home, closed the door of my room and turned on my synthesizer. It was there I would worship the Lord with music. For hours I would become lost in the Spirit, singing the songs of the Lord. I can understand how my parents thought I had gone "bonkers" when they heard all that noise coming out of my room.

During that time I developed a deep relationship with God, and He began to flow through me with what I now know as a prophetic anointing.

How did I know my conversion was real? Never in my life had I developed a passion for anything that compared to my love for God. The pull was more powerful than rock music, more potent than any drug and stronger than the lure of the world. Nothing could compare with the anointing of God's Spirit. It was pure heaven.

At the end of that year Peter gave me some devastating news. "Leslie and I are moving back to Durban." It broke my heart because he was the only one who really encouraged me. Other members of the church didn't see the same potential in me. Suddenly, I was alone, without a friend.

When he left, I went to the pastor and told him I would do anything possible to serve the church. I thought he might say, "Kim, I believe the time has come for you to lead the singing," or "Would you be interested in teaching a Sunday school class?"

Instead he asked if I could help clean the building each

week. "Of course I will" was my response. I began my ministry of sweeping the sanctuary, washing the windows and cleaning the commodes.

I left my job at the factory and started to work as a salesman. I never thought of a career, however. The message of the church was that the Lord's return was so imminent that we should not concern ourselves with earthly pursuits or ambitions. I didn't argue with that application of Scripture — or with anything else that was unique to the church. I knew that God had planted me there for a purpose, and I was determined to learn what it was.

Waiting in the Hallway

During my second year as a Christian, I went to Pastor Pretorius and said, "Sir, I feel that I am ready to attend Bible college and would like you to help me get in."

"I don't believe you are called to the ministry," he replied. "But I'll arrange for you to meet with some of the church officials."

We drove to the headquarters of the denomination in Pretoria, the capital city of South Africa. It was more than six hundred miles from Uitenhage. After my interview I waited in the hallway for nearly three hours while they discussed my potential and finished their other business. Finally, one of the men came out and said, "I know you won't like to hear this, but, young man, we don't believe you are cut out to become a minister."

During my third year at that church I decided to try again. "Please, pastor," I said, "can't you convince the officials that I need to be in Bible school? I know God has called me."

Once again we traveled to the church headquarters. I prepared for the interview by asking the pastor everything I could about doctrine and theology. I also got a fresh haircut and put on my most conservative clothes.

This time Pastor Pretorius said, "Gentlemen, this is a good man. I've never been convinced that he should be a minister, but he thinks God has called him. Why don't you give him a chance?"

The denominational leaders questioned my position on everything from eternal security to Pentecostal manifestations. And I thought I gave the right answers. After a rather lengthy exchange, they said, "We'd like you to wait outside."

When they had made a decision, they came out to me and said, "Kim, we know you love the Lord, but we're still persuaded that you will never become a pastor or an evangelist. You would just be wasting your time pursuing it."

I was distraught. When I returned home I fell on my face before God and cried out: "Lord, is it over? Have I spent three years here for nothing? Didn't I hear Your voice when I was baptized? Didn't You call me to the ministry?"

Not knowing where else to turn for help, I sat down one day and did something quite unusual. I handwrote a letter to Oral Roberts in Tulsa, Oklahoma. I had read his book *Seed Faith,* and I believed he could help me.

"Dear Brother Roberts," I began, "my name is Kim Clement. God has called me to the ministry, and I am asking for your help. I have been rejected twice by the board of a denominational Bible college. My pastor has even told me that I am not truly called, and you may feel the same way. However, I want you to pray about my request. I need to study and prepare myself for what God has planned for my life. I have no way of attending a Bible college, and I cannot afford it. I would appreciate any help or direction you can give me."

With the letter I enclosed a cash gift of five *rand* — or about two dollars.

About one month later I received boxes and boxes of books from the religion department of Oral Roberts University — textbooks, Bible handbooks, commentaries, workbooks and inspirational volumes. I couldn't believe it!

Every day I spent hours devouring the pages of those marvelous books. I could now identify things I had experienced and say, "That happened to me!" or "I didn't know that was in the Bible!"

Oral Roberts had planted a seed in me, and those books confirmed my call and enlarged my vision.

Miracle on the Monument

One night I was awakened from my sleep at about two o'clock in the morning. It was as if the Lord had tapped me on the shoulder. "Go up to the monument and pray," I heard Him say in my spirit.

I walked over to the window and saw that rain was pouring down outside. "Are You sure, Lord?" I asked.

But then I was wide awake, and I sensed an urgency about what God was telling me to do. I put on my raincoat and began to walk up the hill. It was the same park I had escaped to when I was taking drugs and skipping school a few years earlier.

The hill is quite steep. Just in front of the monument to King George V is a fence with an iron gate. That night the gate was locked, and I wasn't sure what to do. I said, "Lord, didn't You ask me to go up to the monument and pray? Well, that's where I'm headed." And I climbed over the fence.

When I cleared the fence and dropped back on the ground, I sensed the presence of the Lord in such an awesome way that I began to cry. As I followed the lighted path to the top of the hill, the Lord seemed so close that I could reach out and touch Him. I was praying out loud and conversing with Him.

As the rain continued to fall, I reached the top of the hill and was about to walk up the steps to the monument.

Suddenly, I heard a loud commotion coming from the direction of the gate. As I turned around, I saw two huge men running toward me. *Lord, You haven't brought me here to kill me now, have You?* I thought in panic.

When the men came closer I could see they were uniformed guards and had police batons in their hands. They stopped me and said, "Do you have any identification? We are security police."

I was so startled I hardly knew what to say.

"What are you doing here?" they wanted to know. "Didn't you see that the fence was locked? We've had drug dealing here, and we want to know what you're up to."

"I'm actually doing nothing," I said as I stood there in the rain. "I'm just praying."

They continued questioning. "Mister, we will let you go if you can tell us where the person is who was walking up the hill with you."

"Listen," I said. "I promise you there was no one else but me. I just wanted to come up here and pray."

Both of them were adamant. "Look, we saw two of you walking up this pathway, and we are going to find the other man."

By this time I was getting curious. "What did the other man look like?" I asked.

"He was slightly taller than you. We saw the two of you talking while you walked up this hill," said one of the policemen. "Don't move. Stay right here. We're going to find him."

For nearly thirty minutes they searched the entire area and could find no one. When they returned I said, "Look, fellows, I know this sounds crazy, but that was Jesus you saw."

"Mister, you must be out of your head."

I returned home soaking wet but praising God. I realized this was a proof that the Lord was with me every step of the way.

The Big Concert

I knew it would be futile to wait another year and knock on the door of the denomination once again. I met with the pastor and said, "At least let me go out and present a concert. That's something I know how to do. I believe it could really minister to people."

For three years I had obeyed the Lord, the church and those He had placed in my life. And more than once I had recalled those early words of the pastor telling me that if I would be faithful, "we will build your character and drive this rebellion out of you."

That is what happened. My defiance of authority had been replaced with a deep love for the Word and for worship. I thought, *Perhaps this church has been the Bible college I needed.*

The church had experienced some changes along with me. Instead of a congregation of seventy-five, it was now filled to its capacity of four hundred. People were driving in from all over the region. It was quite phenomenal.

The more I thought about it, the more I realized how vital it had been to be "rejected" from active ministry. I recalled how the disciples spent three years at the feet of Jesus before they were released to do His work.

I also knew what happened to singer Bob Dylan, who made a profession of faith and was rushed into the Christian spotlight without becoming grounded in the Word. It was like trying to build a tall building without a strong foundation. His commitment crumbled.

Pastor Pretorius finally answered, "Kim, you are right. I think the time has come. I'm all in favor of your doing a concert, and we will sponsor it."

I found a neutral auditorium where young people from the city would feel comfortable. Several of my old band members had now been saved, and we began practicing together. The songs were patterned after those of Andrae

Crouch, who influenced my music tremendously. As we practiced for the concert, I thought, *Wouldn't it be something if I became the white Andrae Crouch?*

Oh, what a difference it was to be playing music for the Lord! We printed hundreds of handbills and flyers announcing Kim Clement and the Righteous Judeans. There were eight of us in the band.

When I entered the auditorium that night, I was shocked by the size of the crowd. The place was packed simply through word of mouth. The news had spread through the rock crowd: "Kim is back into music. He's doing a concert!"

Just before walking onto that stage, I couldn't help but think that it was the beginning of my music ministry. Everything was planned. We had rehearsed twelve songs, and I could almost envision the standing ovation we would receive when the night was over.

It was a mixed crowd — half from the church and half from the world. The sound system was powerful. The lighting effects were superb, and everything ran smoothly for the first two or three songs. Then the event turned into total *chaos.*

Something happened to me that I never could have planned or expected. I abandoned the prepared program and began singing the song of the Lord under a heavy anointing. It was *His* song, His melody, His words — not something I had rehearsed.

I was so used to ministering *to* Him that when it came to entertainment, I couldn't do it anymore. I just started flowing in God's Spirit, and He took over the meeting. The band members were in total shock, and so was I.

While I was worshipping the Lord at the piano, people were being "slain in the Spirit." Some were lying on the floor; some were worshipping God in a heavenly language. Teens were coming to the edge of the stage for salvation. At one point I jumped off the platform and started praying for people. They were coming forward, and all heaven broke loose. It was a wonderful mess.

Then I began to prophesy. God was giving me words for the people, and I delivered them — giving specific words to specific people.

I glanced over at Pastor Pretorius and the leaders from our church, and their eyes were as big as saucers. I could only wonder what they thought. Well, I didn't understand it myself. I thought we would play our songs and have the crowd cheering. And when I would say, "Good night, and God bless you," they would clap for more. But that's not how it turned out.

It was clear that God was moving in my life. But a concert ministry? It was doubtful that would ever happen.

"That's an Order!"

The next invitation I received was not from a church. It was a call for duty in the South African army. It wasn't totally unexpected since every young man was required to do a stint in military service. So when I was twenty-one years old, I was stationed at a camp near the town of Bethlehem in Orange Free State.

It was a great experience because I went as a Christian and viewed it as an opportunity to serve the Lord. Physically, it was demanding. Spiritually, however, it was much tougher than I imagined.

In my off hours I played the piano for some coffee house ministries, and the word got around that I was a fair musician. That's when a high-ranking officer called me and said, "Mr. Clement, we have assigned you to play for a dance at the officers' club next Saturday night."

I was stunned. "No, sir," I said. "I don't play that kind of music."

The officer wasn't used to a new recruit saying no. He let me know that I had refused an order, and the next thing I knew I was sent out to "the hill" with my backpack. I was required to pace the terrain for three or four hours.

The next time I refused to play, the punishment was even harsher. When I was on the ground doing military exercises, a drill sergeant kicked me and broke one of my ribs.

A few days later an army major came to my bunkhouse and said, "Mr. Clement, you will be playing at the officers' club this weekend. That's a direct order."

He meant business. "I will play on one condition," I bargained.

"What's that?"

"That you allow me to play Christian music."

"We can't dance to religious tunes," he huffed.

"Well, I'll show you that you can," I responded with confidence.

That Saturday night I hardly knew what to expect. The club was packed with officers and their decked-out guests. They were definitely in a party mood. When it was my time to play, I went to the piano and began with all the up-tempo songs I could think of. They were dancing to the rhythm of "This Is the Day That the Lord Has Made," "The Lord Liveth" and "Blessed Be the Rock."

They'd be shocked if they knew the words to these songs, I thought with a smile. Later in the evening I slowed the tempo down and began to play the beautiful melody of my favorite worship chorus, "Alleluia."

I closed my eyes and prayed that somehow the Lord would flow through my fingers, through the keyboard, through the strings of that piano and into their hearts.

By the time I had played it the third or fourth time, I could actually feel the Spirit of God enter that room. The loud noise of drinking and dancing had changed into an atmosphere that I could not explain.

"What is that song you are playing?" whispered one of the officers as he came over to the piano. I could see the tears welling up in his eyes.

"It's a song called 'Alleluia,' " I said as I continued to play.

Another officer joined him, and they began asking questions about my background. I told them how Christ had radically transformed my life. Before the evening was over, I was able to pray with both of them and lead them to the Lord. One of them, Major Ivan Graham, then became a wonderful friend.

The Vital Link

When I came out of military service about a year later, I was still at a crossroads regarding God's direction for my future. The only thing I could cling to was the clear voice I heard when I was baptized. I knew in my heart that God had called me to the ministry.

I decided not to go back to the Full Gospel Church of God. Without question my three years there had been ordained by the Lord, but I knew that if I returned, I would once again be locked in with no way to express God's call.

It was rare for pastors to invite me to preach because they didn't understand where the Lord was leading me. They knew what to expect from an evangelist or a teacher, but not from someone with a prophetic ministry. Instead of an outlined sermon with three points and a conclusion, God gave me revelations, and I would share them. Most pastors just couldn't relate to that.

I found a job at a music store in Port Elizabeth, demonstrating and selling pianos, synthesizers and various instruments. At night I was involved in street evangelism in a Christian coffeehouse called the Vital Link. It was an effective ministry to prostitutes, drug addicts and young people who were searching for answers.

One day the phone rang. "Hello. Is this Kim Clement?" asked the voice at the other end of the phone. I was at my office in the music store.

"Yes, it is," I replied. "How can I help you?"

"My name is Pastor Jimmy Crompton," he said. "I am the

pastor of the Pentecostal Protestant Church here in Port Elizabeth. God has told me that you are to join my staff as a minister."

"Sir," I said, "I don't know you. But do you realize that I have no credentials whatsoever? In fact, I have never even finished high school."

"I'm not worried about that at all," he replied. "God told me that you are to come and be our music director and youth pastor."

We arranged to meet at the church, and I knew immediately it was where the Lord wanted me. It was a growing church of about three hundred. And Jimmy Crompton came from a great spiritual heritage. His father had traveled with the remarkable British evangelist Smith Wigglesworth.

As a minister of the Word I left much to be desired, but Jimmy made me feel I was something special in the kingdom of God. He allowed me to express all the things the Lord was giving me, and I was encouraged to be sensitive to the moving of the Holy Spirit in every service. During the times of praise and worship, a mighty anointing would fill the sanctuary, and the entire congregation would begin singing the song of the Lord. Pastor Crompton also had an understanding of prophetic gifts, and he permitted me to use them. What a major role he played in the early stages of my ministry.

A few months after joining the church staff I was invited to play the piano for a meeting of the local Full Gospel Business Men's Fellowship. The guest speaker was Fred Roberts, a well-known pastor from Durban. While I was playing the piano during the early part of the service, I began to lead people in some praise choruses. Over five hundred people lifted their hands and began to worship the Lord. Then Fred Roberts walked over to me and said, "God told me that it's your meeting."

I was startled and told him, "But you don't understand. I'm not a preacher!"

He repeated it again. "It's your meeting. Go for it!" Then he walked back to his seat.

Never before had I been asked to minister to an audience that large. But there was no time to become nervous or afraid. God was present, and I began singing in the Spirit and prophesying — in short, just being God's voice. I preached for about twenty-five minutes and, to my amazement, the altar was lined with people coming to find Christ.

I'm not sure what happened in the lives of those who attended that meeting, but I certainly know what God did for me. If I ever needed a confirmation of God's call, that was it.

Each time after that when Fred Roberts came to our area to speak, he would call me to lead the music. It was obvious that our ministries flowed together in an unusual way. "I'd love for you to come to Durban some time," he told me. "You have an open invitation."

"This Is She!"

Since the moment of my conversion I had not become romantically involved with anyone. It wasn't by chance. The Lord clearly told me that I was not to spend my time looking for a future wife — or even to date. I was so in love with Christ that I didn't care about relationships anyway. He said, "Concentrate on Me. I will bring someone to you, and you will know she is the one when you see her."

One night at the Pentecostal Protestant Church in Port Elizabeth, a young lady walked through the door. Her name was Jane Barnes. She was from a British family in Durban and had traveled to our city to visit a girlfriend who attended our church. Even though she had been raised in a Christian home, she was not living for the Lord. But that night something glorious happened. She was saved and filled with the Spirit.

After the service something else took place. We were

41

introduced to each other. The moment I met her, I said to myself, *This is the one! This is the girl I am going to marry!* I didn't know it at the time, but she was the niece of Fred Roberts.

Jane and I fell deeply in love, and we kept the phone lines busy. I thought I was going to have to get a part-time job to pay for the calls!

A few weeks later I took a weekend off from my duties to visit her in Durban. While I was there, Fred Roberts was conducting a retreat outside the city, so we drove out to see him.

During one of the services a prophetic word was given to me for the second time in my life. The first was at the church in Uitenhage when a visiting minister prayed over me and said, "All I want to say to you, sir, is that God has called you to the ministry." Not even Pastor Pretorious was fully convinced of that, but I claimed those words as from the Lord. Now, at the retreat, God gave me another prophetic word. Someone prayed for me and said, "God is going to move you to Durban."

At first I ignored the word, but it gradually began to witness to my spirit. After I returned to Port Elizabeth, every time I closed my eyes, those words kept coming back. I finally told Pastor Crompton about it, and he said, "If that is what the Lord has planned, I won't stand in your way."

It proved to be the greatest move of my life. Not only did I join the staff of Fred Roberts's church, but a short time later Jane and I were married.

A New Communion

I had only been in Durban for two months when Pastor Roberts called me and the other associate pastor into his office. "God has clearly told me that the racial barriers of ministry must be broken. Spiritually, there must be communion before there can be dominion."

That ran contrary to the rules of the Pentecostal fellowship to which the church belonged. Their policy was to obey the laws of the land. They did not allow blacks in their churches.

Pastor Roberts continued, "I believe we should resign from the denomination, go into the heart of the city and defy the apartheid laws. We should open our doors to every nationality."

It was a huge decision since he had been at the church for many years, and the congregation had grown to several hundred. But it was the right decision.

In 1979 we purchased the Lyric Theater in downtown Durban and opened the doors of the Durban Christian Center. Only a handful attended the first service. Within a few months that handful grew to more than two thousand — Zulus, Xhosas, Bantus, Indians, coloreds, English, Afrikaners — a rainbow of God's people.

Fred Roberts became a mentor to me, and he took great delight in seeing my prophetic ministry grow. His son-in-law Neville Macdonald and his daughter Wendy were also associate ministers and a vital part of the team. Neville later began a multi-racial church in Cape Town, which grew to be the largest congregation in that city.

God was doing marvelous things in the meetings at Durban, and I began to receive invitations from Europe, Australia and the United States. Today the church ministers to more than five thousand each week, and I am still an associate pastor — ministering around the world for nine months each year and preaching in Durban the remaining three, while Pastor Roberts is out conducting crusades.

In 1986 I was traveling in Canada with my family and was scheduled to minister in the United States. One morning I rushed into the airport to pick up my tickets at American Airlines. The woman at the counter said, "Are you Mr. Clement?" She had a concerned look on her face.

"Yes, I am," I replied. "Is there some kind of a problem?"

"I have been asked to give you this message: Your father has died in South Africa."

My heart sank. Then, in a fraction of a second, the Lord said, "Do you remember My word?" My mind flashed back to the voice of God I had heard when I was baptized: "None of your household will go to the grave without salvation." But my father had not been in a right relationship with Christ. I was bewildered.

There in the airport lobby I spoke out loud and told the clerk, "It's impossible! The Lord told me he is not going to die. He's not saved or filled with the Spirit yet."

She had a puzzled look on her face. "Well, I don't know anything about that," she said, "but this is the message I was told to give you. I'm very sorry."

As you'll read later, the word the Lord gave me at my baptism came to pass, though not in the way I expected.

THREE

YOU ARE THE VOICE

M Y LIFE has been filled with surprises.
As a child I expected to become a classical pianist, but that's not what happened. I was on my way to becoming a rock superstar when Jesus came into my life. I dreamed about studying for the ministry, but the Bible college wouldn't admit me. Even when I believed I had found my calling as a professional Christian musician, and presented my first Christian concert, I was able to sing only three songs.

I felt like Jacob, who fell in love with Laban's daughter Rachel. Jacob told Laban, "I will serve you seven years for Rachel your younger daughter" (Gen. 29:18). He endured many hardships during his wait. But on his wedding night when Jacob lifted his bride's veil he found Leah, Laban's firstborn daughter, instead of Rachel.

So often, that is how God works.

During my years "in the desert" at the church in Uitenhage, God stirred something within me that I hadn't sought after and didn't understand. Yet it was there. After being rebuffed and rejected at every turn, I prayed for a word from the Lord about it. At first, I heard only a still, small voice — just a whisper: "I have called you to be a prophet to many nations."

"A *prophet?*" I asked the Lord. "You want me to be a prophet?"

I hardly knew how to define the word, but every time I prayed, the voice grew louder and louder. Finally, with great force, God declared, "I have called you to be a prophet to many nations."

I opened my Bible and read about the specific ministries God gives to the church. "And He Himself gave some to be apostles, some prophets, some evangelists, and some pastors and teachers" (Eph. 4:11). These are called the five-fold ministries.

As I looked around, I saw apostles who provided spiritual leadership, pastors who proclaimed the Word, evangelists who preached to the unsaved and teachers who built up the body of Christ. But where were the prophets?

One person told me that I could read about them in the Old Testament — great prophets like Ezekiel, Daniel, Hosea and Joel.

"No, I am reading the *New* Testament," I told him. "It says there are to be prophets in the church."

It Can't Be Taught

Please understand that I had no desire to become a prophet. The term itself often makes people think that someone is self-appointed and attempting to gain stature in the church. Instead, it was God's specific calling on my life.

But God is raising up prophets today in unprecedented

numbers throughout the world, and you will surely come under the sound of their voices. The Lord may use a prophet to speak directly to you. That's why it is so important to understand the ministry of the prophet today.

If you think this book is going to tell about the dramatic exploits of a prophet who travels the globe telling people about their lives, you will be disappointed. Instead, this book is about *you*. I firmly believe that God desires that the gift of prophecy flow through *millions* of believers. I want you to be prepared when God calls *you* to become His voice.

On these pages we will be examining questions including:

- What is the primary purpose of prophecy?

- Why is God raising up prophets in this generation?

- Is His voice still speaking to us?

- Why are so few people actually receiving the promise of God? (See Acts 2:17-18.)

- Is prophecy for the church, for the world, or for both?

- How can we know God's voice?

- How can we identify a false prophet?

- Does every prophecy have to come true?

When I accepted God's unique call on my life, I began to imagine the great things that God was going to do using this gift. I could actually "see" them. I could visualize myself speaking such truth to people that they would find repentance. I began to dream about giving a word and seeing someone called to the ministry. I even dreamed about *singing* a prophetic utterance that would bring people out of wheelchairs and out of beds of affliction. Then God tugged at my sleeve. It was time to exercise my gift.

Do you remember what happened to Joseph while he was in prison? God gave him the gift of interpreting dreams, but before he approached the Pharaoh, Joseph exercised his prophetic unction on the Pharaoh's chief butler and chief baker. Joseph interpreted each man's dream, and God's word through Joseph came to pass within three days. Two years later Pharaoh had a dream and sent for the young Hebrew. He told Joseph,

> I have dreamed a dream, and there is no one who can interpret it. But I have heard it said of you that you can understand a dream, to interpret it (Gen. 41:15).

Joseph explained that it wasn't *his* power, but God's — *God* would provide the answer. Not only did Joseph become the voice of the Lord, but he was released from prison. The king said, "See, I have set you over all the land of Egypt" (Gen. 41:41).

As I began to exercise my gift, God's voice became clearer and clearer. And the more I understood about prophecy, the bolder a spokesman for the Almighty I became.

A Voice in the Garden

The voice of God is not a new phenomenon. It began at creation.

"God said, 'Let there be light'; and there was light" (Gen. 1:3). How did He create light? He *spoke* it into existence. And that is how He created the earth, vegetation, animal life and mankind. He said it, and it happened.

God created man with His breath.

> And the Lord God formed man of the dust of the
> ground, and breathed into his nostrils the breath
> of life; and man became a living being (Gen. 2:7).

He *spoke* the words, "Be fruitful and multiply" (Gen.
1:28).

God creates by speaking. I believe that one of the basic
principles of prophecy is that God's voice creates something new in our lives. For example, He will supply us with
direction, guidance or knowledge we do not already possess.

The Lord's purpose for Adam and Eve was to give mankind dominion over the earth and fill it with righteousness.
Every day, as they heard God's voice, their knowledge,
wisdom, power and abundance increased. The character of
God was being formed in them. The more they heard, the
more familiar His voice became to them.

God had said to Adam and Eve, "Be fruitful and multiply;
fill the earth and subdue it" (v. 28). If mankind had continued to hear the voice of God, we would have been secure
and creative and had dominion. But Satan realized that we
would overcome him some day, judge him and put him
under our feet. He said, "I must stop them from hearing the
voice of God."

The weapon Satan formed also used the power of words.
He told Adam and Eve, "If you will just partake of that tree
in the midst of the garden you will be exactly like God"
(see Gen. 3:4-5). He tempted them to disobey God, realiz-
ing that if he could cause them to be disobedient they
would become afraid, and the communication between
God and man would stop. But even after Satan lied to Eve
in the garden and they ate of the forbidden fruit, the Lord
continued to speak.

> And they heard the sound of the Lord God walk-
> ing in the garden in the cool of the day, and

Adam and his wife hid themselves from the presence of the Lord God among the trees of the garden (Gen. 3:8).

How did they know it was God? By the sound of His voice.

The Lord always wants to communicate with His people. He asks us questions so we can speak together. "Then the Lord God called to Adam and said to him, 'Where are you?' " (v. 9).

Suddenly, God's voice became frightful to Adam because he had sinned. Adam said, "I heard Your voice in the garden, and I was afraid because I was naked; and I hid myself" (v. 10). For the first time, Adam became aware of his flesh, his nakedness and his limitations.

The voice of the Almighty was no longer a delight to the ear and a joy to the heart. It was terrifying because their natures had changed from righteousness to evil. The purity of His voice caused them to be convicted of their sin. For the first time they experienced the emotions of fear, inferiority and bitterness. Satan also had planted the seeds of pride, arrogance and jealousy. Finally, God banished them from the garden.

Even then, God continued to speak. When we read the first few books of the Old Testament it becomes clear that the Lord was grieved by sin, but the sound of His voice did not diminish. When Cain killed his brother, the Lord said to him, "Where is Abel your brother?" Cain answered, "I do not know. Am I my brother's keeper?" (Gen. 4:9). Cain was so convicted by his lie that he "went out from the presence of the Lord" (v. 16).

"No More!"

Man continued to be fruitful and multiply, but there were only a few righteous men with whom the Lord could communicate. When He found a God-fearing man by the name of Enoch, He literally lifted him out of the earth so they could be together.

> And Enoch walked with God; and he was not, for God took him (Gen. 5:24).

In the history of mankind there have been very few like Enoch, Noah or Abraham who would obey God's voice. Yet He continued to speak. There came a point when the children of Israel said, "No more! We cannot stand hearing His voice any longer." They begged the Almighty to stop speaking to them (see Ex. 20:19 and Heb. 12:19).

God's heart must have been broken. Can you imagine what it would be like if your child told you, "I never want to hear the sound of your voice again because it makes me so fearful"?

What happened next was a turning point in history. For the most part, God had been speaking directly to His people from the time of creation. Then, when God was about to make a covenant with Moses and the children of Israel at Mount Sinai, the Lord called Moses to the top of the mountain and delivered the commandments to him face-to-face (see Ex. 20).

But the voice of God was so powerful that the people in the camp below heard it, too. They became frightened. Moses later described the reaction of the people:

> So it was, when you heard the voice from the midst of the darkness, while the mountain was burning with fire, that you came near to me, all the heads of your tribes and your elders. And you said: "Surely the Lord our God has shown us His glory and His greatness, and we have heard His voice from the midst of the fire. We have seen this day that God speaks with man; yet he still

lives. Now therefore, why should we die? For this great fire will consume us; if we hear the voice of the Lord our God anymore, then we shall die" (Deut. 5:23-25).

They knew that Moses was a righteous man and would be protected by God. But they were sinful and not compatible with God's voice. They said,

For who is there of all flesh who has heard the voice of the living God speaking from the midst of the fire, as we have, and lived? You go near and hear all that the Lord our God may say, and tell us all that the Lord our God says to you, and we will hear and do it (vv. 26-27).

They no longer wanted the responsibility of hearing God's voice. They were saying to Moses, "We don't qualify to hear that voice. You can listen, but not us." The voice presented such a challenge to them that their very flesh reacted negatively — it literally began to die. Instead of hearing from God directly, they now wanted a mediator.

At that point in history God changed the way in which He dealt with man. During the centuries that followed He no longer spoke to man directly, but only through His priests and prophets. The priests would speak to God on behalf of the people, and the prophets would speak to the people on behalf of God.

Man suffered greatly because the direct line of communication had been broken. Many today believe that the rapid decline in longevity began at that moment. Lifespans shrunk from nine hundred years to eight hundred, then three hundred, and finally what we have today.

So how did God speak to His people through prophets?

- The widow's flour and oil did not run dry "according to the word of the Lord which He spoke by Elijah" (1 Kin. 17:16).

- Elisha said to the king's messenger, "Hear the word of the Lord. Thus says the Lord..." (2 Kin. 7:1).

- To an unfaithful Israel, "the Lord began to speak by Hosea..." (Hos. 1:2).

- "The Lord spoke by Isaiah" to the commander of the Assyrian army (Is. 20:2).

- The king of Persia proclaimed liberty for those in exile "that the word of the Lord spoken by the mouth of Jeremiah might be fulfilled" (2 Chron. 36:22).

For hundreds of years God spoke to His people *through* prophets like Ezekiel, Daniel, Hosea, Joel, Amos, Obadiah, Jonah, Micah, Nahum, Habakkuk, Zephaniah, Haggai, Zechariah and Malachi. To the ordinary men and women, the heavens were shut.

When a prophet would come into the city and say, "Hear the word of the Lord," the people would start to tremble. Sometimes they were so convicted that they would say, "Go away! Speak to someone else!"

In many cases the people rejected God's word because they thought it was merely the man who was speaking. The people were under a tremendous bondage and in danger of being manipulated because they had to depend on a man to hear God for them. But what else could they do? The windows of heaven had been closed.

Arrival of the Word

Then it happened. The greatest fulfillment of prophecy

took place when Christ broke through the heavenlies and was born in Bethlehem. God said, "It is time for Me to send My Word to the earth."

Jesus was that Word.

> In the beginning was the Word, and the Word was with God, and the Word was God...And the Word became flesh and dwelt among us, and we beheld His glory, the glory as of the only begotten of the Father, full of grace and truth (John 1:1,14).

What a momentous event! No longer would a prophet of flesh and blood be necessary for people to hear from God. Christ was the *living* Word.

The priests of the day were angry because someone had invaded their territory. They wouldn't accept John the Baptist being the voice of God and prophesying the coming of Jesus. "Who are you?" they wanted to know (v. 19).

John replied in the words of the prophet Isaiah,

> [I am] "the voice of one crying in the wilderness: 'Make straight the way of the Lord' " (v. 23).

John eventually baptized the Messiah who he predicted would come. When Jesus came out of the water, something fantastic happened in the supernatural realm.

> The heavens were opened to Him, and He saw the Spirit of God descending like a dove and alighting upon Him. And suddenly a voice came from heaven, saying, "This is My beloved Son, in whom I am well pleased" (Matt. 3:16-17).

Jesus' baptism marked four important events: 1) The Word had come to the earth; 2) the heavens were opened;

3) the Spirit descended; and 4) a voice came from heaven.

The moment God sends His word to your heart, the Spirit alights upon that word and becomes the voice. It's actually the Spirit doing it, not us. He uses our mouths to voice what the word has already said.

After that event, Jesus' words resulted in great miracles. When the seas churned, He spoke the word and said, "Peace, be still," and the waters calmed (Mark 4:39). When Lazarus had been dead for four days, Christ knew that His voice had the power to raise him. Jesus walked to the tomb and cried with a loud voice, "Lazarus, come forth!" And Lazarus came forth, alive and still wrapped in his grave-clothes (John 11:43-44). Life was restored by the power of His voice.

A great transformation had taken place in the world! Man's disobedience had caused sin to appear, and that led to God speaking only through an intermediary. So Satan did everything possible to make God's prophets and priests disobedient — and sometimes he was successful.

Now, the obedience of one man — Jesus Christ — opened up the heavens. God was once again speaking directly to His people.

It should not be surprising that Satan led Jesus to the mount of temptation. If Christ could be made disobedient, He would become like the rest of mankind. But the Lord was faithful unto death.

> [Christ] for the joy that was set before Him endured the cross, despising the shame (Heb. 12:2).

Revealed From Heaven

Peter was one of the first who heard God's voice for himself.

When Jesus came into the region of Caesarea

Philippi, He asked His disciples, saying, "Who do men say that I, the Son of Man, am?"

So they said, "Some say John the Baptist, some Elijah, and others Jeremiah or one of the prophets."

He said to them, "But who do you say that I am?" (Matt. 16:13-15).

After being raised in a culture in which people felt unqualified to hear directly from heaven, the disciples were hesitant to answer. Then Peter found enough courage to say, "You are the Christ, the Son of the living God" (v. 16). Jesus replied,

> Blessed are you, Simon Bar-Jonah, for flesh and blood has not revealed this to you, but My Father who is in heaven (v. 17).

Because Peter had entered into a dimension of divine communication with the Father, Jesus said to him,

> On this rock I will build My church, and the gates of Hades shall not prevail against it. And I will give you the keys of the kingdom of heaven, and whatever you bind on earth will be bound in heaven, and whatever you loose on earth will be loosed in heaven (vv. 18-19).

Since Jesus Christ restored divine communication, are the heavens now open all the time? No. They can be blocked by spiritual wickedness. Thus, we have been given the power to bind or loose things on earth and in heaven in accordance with God's voice as He speaks to us.

Christ was the Word of the Father. He told His disciples, "He who has seen Me has seen the Father" (John 14:9). "The words that I speak to you I do not speak on My own authority; but the Father who dwells in Me does the works" (v. 10).

Then Christ gave this promise: "Most assuredly, I say to you, he who believes in Me, the works that I do he will do also; and greater works than these he will do, because I go to My Father" (v. 12).

He was saying, "I am going back to the Father, but *you* will become the voice of God." Christ was the Word of the Father, but we were to become the voice of that Word.

Later, when the Spirit descended at Pentecost, "They were all filled with the Holy Ghost, and began to speak with other tongues, as the Spirit gave them utterance" (Acts 2:4, KJV).

The Spirit breathes on the Word and gives it a voice. When Peter came out of the upper room and began to preach the gospel, he literally became the voice of God. It wasn't really Peter that was preaching; it was the Spirit bringing forth the word.

The Pharisees once asked Jesus when the kingdom of God would come. Jesus replied,

> The kingdom of God does not come with obser-
> vation; nor will they say, "See here!" or "See
> there!" For indeed, the kingdom of God is within
> you (Luke 17:20-21).

Jesus was pointing out once again that a great change had taken place in the spiritual realm. No longer would God selectively communicate to chosen individuals. He would reveal His kingdom in the heart of anyone who would believe.

An Open Door

The purpose of a prophet today is drastically changed from the prophet's purpose in Old Testament times when they often pronounced judgment or predicted future events. Though on some occasions New Testament prophets do those things, that is not their primary role.

After years of ministering the prophetic word, I have come to understand the role of prophecy for today. When the voice of the Lord speaks, it is as if a door of opportunity has been opened. The Lord often presents a message concerning how the person should live. The word reveals the desire of God's heart — what He wants for that person. But if that person refuses to walk through the door God has created for them, he or she will not see His revelation fulfilled.

Most people have no concept of how God speaks today. I cannot count the times that sincere people have asked me questions such as, Should I marry the person I am now dating? Will I get a promotion at my job? Will my mother die from the cancer in her body?

A prophet is not a diviner of future events. God uses him or her to express what He wants to say, not what someone wants to hear.

A man in Texas recently approached me and said, "Kim, would you pray for me? I need a word from God."

I felt that this man had a good relationship with the Lord, so I said, "Why should I pray for you for a word from the Lord?"

He looked startled until I explained, "You have the same access to God's throne that I have." As a child of God he could hear the voice of God as clearly as I could.

It is time for the church to realize that every Christian should become an instrument in the hands of the Lord — receiving His clear and mighty word.

You don't *need* a prophet for every decision of your life. Instead, see yourself as the voice of God. God communicates directly to His people. But He may send a prophet to confirm what He has already spoken to you in your secret place of prayer.

The Bible speaks of the two voices of God — His voice in the heavens and His voice on earth. The writer of Hebrews says, "See that you do not refuse Him who speaks. For if they did not escape who refused Him who spoke on earth, much more shall we not escape if we turn away from Him who speaks from heaven" (Heb. 12:25).

Today, the Lord Himself speaks to us, though He may send a prophet to confirm it as His words.

When Jesus was baptized in water at the river Jordan, the Father spoke to Him from heaven and said, "This is My beloved Son, in whom I am well pleased" (Matt. 3:17). Then, thirteen chapters later, the Lord asked His disciples, "Who do you say that I am?" (Matt. 16:15). Peter answered, "You are the Christ, the Son of the living God" (v. 16).

Peter confirmed what the Father told Jesus at His baptism. That is why Jesus told the disciple, "Flesh and blood has not revealed this to you, but My Father who is in heaven" (v. 17).

The Lord desires us to become the voice of God. Christ has broken down the partition that once existed between the Father and us. The Holy Spirit has been released on the earth. Jesus "has made us kings and priests to His God and Father" (Rev. 1:6).

People constantly ask, "Kim, do you actually hear audible words when God speaks to you?" That has happened on occasions, but the vast majority of the time He speaks to my spirit, and I have learned to recognize His voice. God certainly has the capability of speaking with an audible voice. But those who tell you they have heard "the voice of God" will almost always say that the communication has been Spirit to spirit.

How is it possible for the Lord to speak to our inner man? Let's look at the way God created man — as a spirit being who resides in a physical body of flesh and blood. "And the Lord God formed man of the dust of the ground, and breathed into his nostrils the breath of life; and man became a living being" (Gen. 2:7). God breathed His Spirit into man so that he would become compatible with the Father. As a result, God can speak Spirit to spirit since He has no dealings with the flesh. That is why the Lord can speak to us spiritually, and we can understand what He is saying.

However, something more needs to happen to be able to recognize God's voice. We need to be reconciled to God by accepting His Son as our Savior. Doing this creates an open channel between the Father and us. From that moment on we are able to hear the spiritual word of the Lord. It is something that a person cannot hear with the natural ear.

After we intensely listen and digest what He is saying, we are to tell the world. We not only hear His word, but become the voice of that word.

When you become receptive to the voice of God, you are like a soldier who has been given a great weapon. You are equipped to conquer every obstacle that comes your way.

I'm not talking about opening your Bible each morning and reading a few passages, although that is important. I'm talking about taking time for God's Word to come alive in your life — not only in your thoughts and deeds, but through your voice as well.

A Familiar Voice

The Bible says, "Let everyone who can hear, listen to what the Spirit is saying" (Rev. 2:17, TLB). Our great concern should not be how the Spirit has directed us in the past, but what the Lord is saying now.

As you continue to read these pages you will understand that God is speaking all the time. If you will take the opportunity to listen, He will do great and marvelous things in your life. You will not only receive insights about His will for your future, but He will show you how to live *now*. It is a supernatural lifestyle the world craves but cannot attain until it turns its ears toward that wonderful sound.

When our son, Caleb, was a small baby we would put him in the nursery of the church while I conducted a service. As often happens when a child is in the presence of strangers, he would become irritated and aggravated with the other children. One night, at the end of a long service, I saw someone bring him into the back of the auditorium. The moment he heard the sound of my voice his entire disposition changed. He instantly was transformed from a miserable little lad into an excited child.

My voice was familiar; a sound that instinctively gave him comfort and security. He didn't need to see me or even touch me. The sound of his father's voice was all that he needed. If he could have expressed how he felt, I'm sure he would have said, "Everything's going to be all right now."

Many people believe that the glory of God is seen only through signs, wonders and miracles, which are certainly ordained of the Lord. But I believe God's glory and greatness are revealed when He chooses to speak to you and me through the magnificent sound of His voice.

Some folks pray that the Lord will somehow come down from His throne and visit them. But as you serve Him, He will draw you to where He is — the holy of holies on the mount of the Lord. As a believer you have access into the heavenly realm of God.

Invading His Territory

The battle for the heavenlies is still being waged.

> For we do not wrestle against flesh and blood,
> but against principalities, against powers, against
> the rulers of the darkness of this age, against

spiritual hosts of wickedness in the heavenly places (Eph. 6:12).

The conflict will not end until Christ "delivers the kingdom to God the Father, when He puts an end to all rule and all authority and power" (1 Cor. 15:24). Satan will be "cast into the lake of fire and brimstone" (Rev. 20:10).

Satan, whom Scripture calls "the prince of the power of the air" (Eph. 2:2), is terrified when we become the voice of God. Our very breath has invaded his territory. That is why we need to vocalize what is in our spirits.

Jesus taught that speaking and believing go hand in hand. He said,

> For assuredly, I say to you, whoever says to this mountain, "Be removed and be cast into the sea," and does not doubt in his heart, but believes that those things he says will come to pass, he will have whatever he says. Therefore I say to you, whatever things you ask when you pray, believe that you receive them, and you will have them (Mark 11:23-24).

Why are we to speak it? Not because we need to be persuaded; nor does God need to be convinced. It is because the kingdoms of darkness need to be terrorized by the voice of Almighty God. You are the instrument of God's voice.

You may ask, "Why should God use me? I'm just an ordinary person." If you are a member of the body of Christ and have received His Spirit, the breath of God resides in you. He has given you the ability to communicate for one great purpose. Through your vocal cords He can speak to the world. Instead of asking why God should use you, ask, what does He want you to say.

The glory of the gospel is this: We have the Word with

us. And as we will see, when the Word resides in our spirits, we can become the voice of Almighty God.

How will you respond when the Lord gives you a word? What will you do when the Spirit begins to breathe on you? Will you open your mouth and become His voice?

The moment God gives you something He wants you to say, don't hesitate. Speak it out. Suddenly the heavens will open, and Satan will flee.

Always remember that Jesus is the Word, the Holy Spirit is the breath, and you are the voice of God.

FOUR

THE PROMISE
OF TOMORROW

WE BELIEVE that you have the word of the Lord, and we have something we want you to pray about," said the pastor from Alberta, Canada, who had phoned me.

"What is it?" I asked him.

"I don't believe we should tell you," he replied. "You just pray that God will reveal it."

I had already agreed to come to his church, and now I was wondering what kind of a situation I was walking into. All I could do was pray.

For several days before I flew to Alberta, I sought God for a special word. "Lord," I prayed, "I need to hear from You. What is the message You have for this congregation?"

Then, while I was on my face before the Lord, He spoke

to my spirit and said, "There is a woman in the church who is causing tremendous discord and unrest." But God gave me more than a word. He also showed me her face.

On Sunday morning when I walked to the platform for my first service, I looked out at the audience, and there she was — the same face I had seen in prayer. The woman was seated on the fourth row at the end by the aisle. Her husband was next to her.

The pastor had just introduced me when I felt something inside say, "Do it now. Do it now!"

Please, Lord, I prayed, *these people hardly know me.*

But I obeyed the urging of the Spirit, stepped down from the platform and walked over to the woman. "Please stand up," I said to her. And the moment I said those words an uncomfortable hush came over the congregation. Everyone was motionless — all attention was riveted on what was about to happen.

"God says that you are fearful of airplanes," I said.

"Yes, I am," the woman said as she looked over at her husband. They seemed happy that I knew.

"The Lord tells me that you are going to get on an airplane. It's a little one with two engines. And God is going to fly you over the snow, toward Alaska."

I continued delivering the message the Lord was giving me. "There has been trouble, but you have been faithful. God says, 'The time has come now, and I am going to release you from this place.' "

After the service, while I was having lunch with the pastor, he said, "Kim, you have no idea how God used you this morning."

"Tell me about it," I said.

He told me that woman and her husband were the founders of the church. Because of that, they felt like they could make decisions for everyone in the congregation — including the minister and his wife. "You'll never know the concern it has caused," he said. "We have been on the verge of resigning for several months."

A short time later I learned that the couple moved to Alaska. Yes, they flew. And when they left the church, the woman and her husband were happy and rejoicing.

Can you imagine what would have happened in the service in Alberta if I had said, "You know you are a bunch of troublemakers, and you need to get out of here"?

Some people want to hear prophets like that. They are so sick of the devil they would like to see old Ezekiel with his long robes declaring:

> Now the end has come upon you,
> And I will send My anger against you;
> I will judge you according to your ways,
> And I will repay you for all your abominations
>   (Ezek. 7:3).

That is how God spoke through Old Testament prophets, but we are living in a new day. If I had vented a rebuke in anger, the woman could have easily rebelled. The church would have been torn apart, and the work of the Lord would have suffered.

I will never forget that experience because it brought into focus three important principles regarding the use of prophecy today. The Lord is still creative and can speak in any manner He chooses, but in almost every instance the following is true:

1. Prophecy is for the church.

2. Prophecy is to be given in love.

3. Prophecy presents a promise of God.

A Word for the World?

I am often asked, "Whom is God addressing when He gives a prophetic word? Is He speaking to the church? Or is the message for the world?"

The prophet is primarily directed to give a word to the body of Christ. Scripture tells us that "tongues are for a sign, not to those who believe but to unbelievers; but prophesying is not for unbelievers but for those who believe" (1 Cor. 14:22).

But there are times when God uses prophecy as a means of evangelism to witness to the unredeemed. Paul said that if people prophesy "and an unbeliever or an uninformed person comes in, he is convinced by all, he is judged by all. And thus the secrets of his heart are revealed; and so, falling down on his face, he will worship God and report that God is truly among you" (vv. 24-25).

Each of the fivefold ministries we discussed earlier has a distinct purpose (Eph. 4:11). The *evangelist* has been called as a soul winner. The *teacher* is expected to instruct. The *apostle* is appointed to govern. The *pastor* is required to shepherd and nurture the church. But the *prophet* is to be the voice of God to the believer.

The ultimate purpose of prophecy is to fulfill the Great Commission, but that happens when the Lord speaks first to the redeemed. When believers hear from God, they are equipped to bring unbelievers to Christ. That's God plan. The church must come to repentance before it can bring the world to the cross.

Since God speaks to the world *through* believers, it is vital that we not only hear, but speak, His word. If the redeemed of the Lord hear that sound from heaven but refuse to speak it, the message will never be heard on earth. Scripture warns us:

See that you do not refuse Him who speaks. For

if they did not escape who refused Him who spoke on earth, much more shall we not escape if we turn away from Him who speaks from heaven (Heb. 12:25).

I believe there is another reason why the Lord declared that prophecy is for the church. A believer will receive God's word and act upon it. But an unbeliever will often begin to revere the prophet and miss the message he brings.

A Heart of Love

The word God gives you must be spoken within the character and personality of Jesus. If not, the message will fail — no matter how accurate it is.

What is the heart and personality of Christ? It is love. He said, "A new commandment I give to you, that you love one another; as I have loved you, that you also love one another" (John 13:34).

Many times I have seen a prophet state truth so arrogantly that it is not effective. The Bible says, "A wicked messenger falls into trouble, but a faithful ambassador brings health" (Prov. 13:17).

The moment you say, "thus says the Lord," you are representing God in speech. If He gives you the word, He will also let you know how He is *feeling* about the person to whom you are speaking.

In Old Testament times, when a ruler sent a message to another land, the spokesman would make every effort to deliver it in the same tone in which it was given to him. If his master felt great sorrow, that's what the messenger would express. If the king had laughed, the ambassador would laugh, too.

That same method needs to be used in prophetic ministry. When you speak the word of the Lord, deliver it in the tone you received it from the Lord. Do you remember when Moses misrepresented God by striking the rock to produce water? God had ordered him to *speak* to it. "Take the rod; you and your brother Aaron gather the assembly together. Speak to the rock before their eyes, and it will yield its water" (Num. 20:8). A word was all that was necessary.

But how can we be certain we are operating in perfect love? A prophet must be:

- Slow to suspect, quick to trust

- Slow to condemn, quick to justify

- Slow to expose, quick to shield

- Slow to reprimand, quick to forbear

- Slow to belittle, quick to appreciate

- Slow to demand, quick to give

- Slow to hinder, quick to help

- Slow to provoke, quick to conciliate

- Slow to resent, quick to forgive

I have made mistakes during the years God has used me in the ministry of prophecy — especially when I have become too emotionally involved in the situation.

Let me give you an example. God once showed me a man in the congregation who was committing adultery. Immediately I found that I was becoming furious with him. If I had marched up to him belligerently and said, "Sir, you are being unfaithful to your wife," the results would have been disastrous. His wife would have been humiliated, and he would have been angry with both God and me. The man might have stopped committing adultery, but it is doubtful that he would have repented from his heart.

The prophet doesn't have to say precisely what is going on in someone's life. The person hearing the prophecy will know what the prophet is talking about. A word from the Lord that only approaches the subject can still pierce their heart like an arrow. Scripture tells us that "the goodness of God leads you to repentance" (Rom. 2:4).

Used Watches

More than once I have been accused of being a "compromising" prophet because I have refused to publicly expose sin. One well-meaning man accused me by saying, "We know you have been to churches where there is sin taking place, and you have not revealed it."

I responded by telling him that God has directed me to speak truth by demonstrating the fruit of the Spirit — love, joy, peace and gentleness. And restoration has taken place in hundreds of lives. Openly exposing sin can cause fear to enter a church and hearts to become hardened. In that case, people will continue in their wicked ways. But when the spirit of a church is transformed from condemnation to love, there is repentance.

How should a prophet respond if God says, "Sam, the jeweler is a crook. He is selling reconditioned watches and representing them as new"?

Again, the manner in which a prophet delivers the message is important. He or she could go to the jeweler and blatantly reveal the truth by saying, "You're a crook. You are selling used watches as if they were new."

That may stop the wrongdoing, but his heart will not be transformed. Since God brings judgment to those who refuse to repent, you have brought trouble into his life.

How much better to say in his presence, "I know about a jeweler who sells reconditioned watches as if they were new." Expose sin gently and with love. Which is more important? Being specific or producing repentance?

There are times, however, when God may direct you to confront sin in an unusual manner.

> Jesus went into the temple and began to drive out those who bought and sold in the temple, and overturned the tables of the money changers (Mark 11:15).

That's how He demonstrated His love and respect for the house of God.

When you hear the voice of the Lord, respond — no matter what He tells you to do. Jesus said,

> The works which the Father has given Me to finish — the very works that I do — bear witness of Me, that the Father has sent Me (John 5:36).

I will always remember a service I conducted in Australia. There was a large crowd in the auditorium. On the front row was a man who had his hands raised, praising the Lord. God spoke to me and said, "That man is molesting little children. He is obsessed with pornography and is selling it."

When that was revealed to me, I thought, *How horrible. He is mixing what is profane with what is sacred.*

Suddenly anger arose within me. Immediately I ran down and did something I had never done before. I started slapping the back of his hands with short but stinging slaps. I didn't have to say a word, though my flesh was tempting me. The man began to weep uncontrollably, and true repentance came into his life.

When Jesus talked with the woman at the well, He knew everything about her life, but He used great discretion in choosing His words.

> Jesus said to her, "Go, call your husband, and come here."

The woman answered and said, "I have no husband."

Jesus said to her, "You have well said, 'I have no husband,' for you have had five husbands, and the one whom you now have is not your husband; in that you spoke truly" (John 4:16-18).

The Lord actually complimented her for the half-truth she told. He didn't say, "You lied." Instead he said, "Well spoken, but..." Then He told her the truth which set her free.

A prophet must know more than what to say; he must know how to say it. Jesus said, "Behold, I send you out as sheep in the midst of wolves. Therefore be wise as serpents and harmless as doves" (Matt. 10:16)

God's Great Promise

When God speaks, He gives a remarkable preview of what His people can expect. He talks about today and tomorrow, not yesterday. And many times He reveals His plans first to a prophet.

God has the power to do whatever He chooses, but He has given much of the responsibility to us. Whom did He ask to "be fruitful and multiply; fill the earth and subdue it; have dominion over...every living thing that moves on the earth"? (Gen. 1:28) He gave that assignment to you and me through Adam and Eve.

The prophetic ministry is a ministry of hope. It presents a divine revelation of God's dream for tomorrow. Rarely does the prophet tell you specific steps you must take to reach the goal. He simply tells you what God wants for your future and then departs.

It is left to the pastor or the teacher to tell you, "This is what you must do to reach that objective."

As a spokesman for the Lord I have been given a wonderful assignment. I deliver God's good news and then go on my way. Some people have the image of a prophet as one who is somber and angry — lashing out at unrighteousness. But they are thinking about Old Testament prophets, not those whom God is calling today.

You may ask, "Is a prophecy always fulfilled? Is it possible for a word from the Lord not to come to pass?"

If God says, "I will," you can rest assured that is exactly what He plans to do. But there are conditions He requires on our parts. They include faith, belief and the act of receiving. If we choose not to follow through on the conditions, the promise remains for our descendants.

I believe this is exactly how God works. Unfortunately, most people don't believe He means what He says. The Lord may deliver a word that says, "I'm going to heal you" or "I'm going to provide for you." Immediately that person may have an identity crisis and think, "I am not worthy. I'm still doing things that are wrong. This can't be God speaking to me!"

Here is what the Bible declares:

Therefore, as the Holy Spirit says:

> "Today, if you will hear His voice,
> Do not harden your hearts as in the
> rebellion,
> In the day of trial in the wilderness,
> Where your fathers tested Me, proved
> Me,
> And saw My works forty years" (Heb.
> 3:7-9).

If you want God's promise for tomorrow, here is what to do right now: "*Today*...do not harden your hearts."

He leaves the choice to you.

To put it another way, if you harden your heart, today

remains today and tomorrow will never come. God speaks *now* to prepare you for the future.

How to Enter Tomorrow

Why do people turn a deaf ear to God's voice? Because they do not know how the Lord operates. It was exactly the same with the children of Israel. The Lord said, "They always go astray in their heart, and they have not known My ways" (v. 10).

When God says, "I'm going to heal your disease," and the doctor says, "I'm giving you three months to live," most people say, "I don't see how God can make a way." They think God can't do it — and they turn away from God's voice. Why? Because they receive the natural voice easier than the spiritual voice.

The message is clear. The generation of Israelites that hardened their hearts and refused the Lord's promise stayed exactly where they were. God said, "They shall not enter My rest" (v. 11).

When you don't receive the promise, time stands still, and you don't enter tomorrow. That is how God works. He waits to see the condition of your heart.

> And to whom did He swear that they would not enter His rest, but to those who did not obey? So we see that they could not enter in because of unbelief (vv. 18-19).

In the early days of Christ's ministry He "went about all Galilee, teaching in their synagogues, preaching the gospel of the kingdom, and healing all kinds of sickness and all kinds of disease among the people" (Matt. 4:23). But what happened when He went to Nazareth, His hometown? "And He did not do many mighty works there because of their unbelief" (Matt. 13:58).

What is the "rest" the Lord spoke of in Hebrews 3? It is a rest from all our enemies. Scripture tells us that there will be a generation that experiences such a deliverance.

When the author of the book of Hebrews wrote these words, no one had entered that rest. God promised it to the children of Israel, but they did not step out in faith and receive it. So the promise remains for you and for me.

> Therefore, since a promise remains of entering His rest, let us fear lest any of you seem to have come short of it (Heb. 4:1).

The promise is not about heaven; it's about now. There is a generation that is to have dominion and subdue illness and iniquity.

What the Bible says next is at the heart of receiving a prophetic word.

> For indeed the gospel was preached to us as well as to them; but the word which they heard did not profit them, not being mixed with faith in those who heard it (v. 2).

Yes, it is possible to receive a word from God and fail to benefit. Why? Because the message has not been combined with faith. It is only those who *believe* who can enter His rest.

> Since therefore it remains that some must enter it, and those to whom it was first preached did not enter because of disobedience, again He designates a certain day, saying in David, "Today," after such a long time, as it has been said:
>
> Today, if you will hear His voice,
> Do not harden your hearts.

For if Joshua had given them rest, then He
would not afterward have spoken of another day
(vv. 6-8).

I believe God is still saying, "Today! Yield your heart to
My word, and I will lead you into tomorrow." Again, the
Bible says, "There remains therefore a rest for the people of
God" (v. 9).

In the Lord's view we are "a chosen generation, a royal
priesthood, a holy nation" (1 Pet. 2:9). God made "Him
who knew no sin to be sin for us, that we might become
the righteousness of God in Him" (2 Cor. 5:21). When we
receive Christ we have "the fullness of the Godhead" (Col.
2:9) because He dwells in us.

It is time to claim our inheritance and enter His rest.

Only a Word

Many people are looking for God to come down from
His throne and provide a miraculous deliverance. Instead,
they need to be saying, "Lord, speak the word!"

A wonderful thing happened when Jesus went to Capernaum on the north shore of the Sea of Galilee. As the Lord
entered the city, "a centurion came to Him, pleading with
Him, saying, 'Lord, my servant is lying at home paralyzed,
dreadfully tormented' " (Matt. 8:5-6).

Then Jesus made an offer that I cannot imagine anyone
refusing. The Lord said, "I will come and heal him" (v. 7).

But the centurion — a Roman military officer in charge
of a hundred soldiers — turned to Christ and said, "Lord, I
am not worthy that You should come under my roof. But
only speak a word, and my servant will be healed" (v. 8).
He didn't want a personal visit — just a word.

It was obvious that the centurion knew more about the
authority of the Lord than many others of his day. The
Jews, the covenant children of God, were void of such

understanding. Even the disciples had difficulty comprehending what Christ meant when He said, "I am the way, the truth, and the life" (John 14:6), and "He who has seen Me has seen the Father" (v. 9). They said among themselves, "What is this that He says to us?" (John 16:17)

The centurion understood the power of the spoken word. He said,

> For I also am a man under authority, having soldiers under me. And I say to this one, "Go," and he goes; and to another, "Come," and he comes; and to my servant, "Do this," and he does it (Matt. 8:9).

The Lord had never been approached in such a manner. Others came seeking His healing touch, but this man wanted only a word.

> When Jesus heard it, He marveled, and said to those who followed, "Assuredly, I say to you, I have not found such great faith, not even in Israel!"
>
> Then Jesus said to the centurion, "Go your way; and as you have believed, so let it be done for you." And his servant was healed that same hour (vv. 10, 13).

The healing took place because the centurion had total faith in the voice of God. Jesus saw his heart and said, "As you have believed, so let it be done."

If you are ready to see the Lord marvel at *your* reaction, start trusting His word and His promises.

In my ministry I meet people every day who are praying for a visitation from the Lord. They want Him to come down from His throne and enter their homes. "Please, Lord," they cry, "come and touch me. Come and heal me!"

That is not how God operates today. Only once did God ever step out of eternity into time. He sent His Son to restore what was destroyed by Satan in the garden. Christ not only took on the physical form of man, but He took our sins to the cross. He died, rose again and ascended to heaven.

Today it is not necessary for God to come to you. Instead, He has made it possible for you to have direct access to heaven. The Lord is saying, "Come and hear what I have to say. And when you hear My word, I'll pull back the curtain of time and show you the future."

When I hear the voice of the Lord, it is as though I am raised to higher ground, hearing the conversation of the Godhead in heavenly places. As the apostle Paul says, God has "raised us up together, and made us sit together in the heavenly places in Christ Jesus" (Eph. 2:6). Isaiah, too, heard the conversation of God when God brought him into His heavenly throne room.

Also I heard the voice of the Lord, saying:

"Whom shall I send,
And who will go for Us?"

Then I said, "Here am I! Send me" (6:8).

I believe we can hear Jesus just as clearly as the apostle John did on the isle of Patmos. God confirmed that through John, saying:

Behold, I stand at the door and knock. If anyone hears My voice and opens the door, I will come in to him and dine with him, and he with Me (Rev. 3:20).

Perhaps you are beginning to know how I can have

confidence when I look at someone and say, "God says you will not die. You will live!"

But when you have a prophetic word from God, you must realize that God has done His part. Now it is up to you. The Lord waits to see if your heart agrees with what He has said.

Whose Prophet Is Greater?

At one of our crusades in South Africa we began to have a large number of Muslims attending the services. More than a thousand attended night after night because they heard a prophet who represented Christ was in their city.

Many in the audience came because, as one man put it, "They wanted to make sure that their prophet is greater than the prophet of Christ."

To me, it was a foolish thing to say because Mohammed is dead.

That night the anointing of the Holy Spirit filled the auditorium. Suddenly I began to call out — by name — unsaved people, specifically Muslims. It was one of the most unique meetings I have ever witnessed.

The Lord gave me the name Ishmael, for example. I called out the name, and Ishmael stood up. I told him his home address and asked, "Is that where you live?" He said, "Yes."

"Ishmael, come to the front," I said. "God wants to tell you something."

When he arrived at the platform, Ishmael said, "But I am a Muslim."

"Well, I am a Christian. And God has given me a word for you. Jesus tells me that your father is dying of liver cancer and he's been given a few months left to live. But Jesus — not only the prophet, but the Son of God — says that you are to go and tell him that he is healed."

79

"Yes. What you say is true," said Ishmael. "I will go and tell him."

Hundreds of Muslims gave their hearts to Christ and prayed the sinner's prayer because of the voice of the Lord. There was such power in His word that on many nights they would literally run to the altar for salvation.

The Lord is not only alive, but He continues to speak to His people.

Opening Heaven's Door

When God spoke to Abraham, Isaac, Jacob and other people in Old Testament times, He nearly always gave them a preview of what was about to happen next. It was to prove to them that the situation they were facing would be overcome.

Today, the Lord also gives us a promise when He speaks to us. He says, "Behold, I stand at the door and knock. If anyone hears My voice and opens the door, I will come in to him and dine with him, and he with Me" (Rev. 3:20).

We usually think of these words in terms of the unsaved. But they also apply to those who are saved. (In fact, the verse was part of a message to the church of Laodicea.) The Lord says "if" we hear His voice and open the door, He will be with us. Not "when," but "if." That same concept appears throughout Scripture.

> If you will indeed obey My voice and keep My covenant, then you shall be a special treasure to Me (Ex. 19:5).

> And the Lord will make you the head and not the tail...if you heed the commandments of the Lord your God (Deut. 28:13).

> If what you heard from the beginning abides in you, you also will abide in the Son and in the Father (1 John 2:24).

The choice is yours: Will you listen to the sound of His voice or not? If you do, then you must take action and spiritually "open" the door. Who opens it? *You* do!

Many people have been raised in an environment of mistrust. They have been wounded by other people so often that when God tries to knock at their door, they are afraid to open it. There is a vast difference, however, between the voice of God and the voice of man. Spend time with the Lord. When you get to know the distinct sound of His voice, your heart will become tender to His call.

> After these things I looked, and behold, a door standing open in heaven. And the first voice which I heard was like a trumpet speaking with me, saying, "Come up here, and I will show you things which must take place after this" (Rev. 4:1).

The voice did not say, "I am coming down to you." It said, "Come up here!"

Then, just as the Lord does for you and me, He gave John a promise. He said, "I will show you things which must take place after this." Tomorrow was about to be revealed.

When God told Abraham to offer Isaac as a sacrifice, God didn't come down from heaven. Instead, Abraham followed the Lord to the mountain. When Isaac was delivered, "Abraham called the name of the place, The-Lord-Will-Provide; as it is said to this day, 'In the Mount of The Lord it shall be provided'" (Gen. 22:14).

The Almighty did not descend from Mount Sinai to meet

Moses. "The Lord called Moses to the top of the mountain, and Moses went up" (Ex. 19:20).

God has not changed. When He wants to speak to you, His voice calls you to where He is.

There is much more to life than a physical world and a human society. God longs to speak to your soul in a heavenly dimension. When you make the choice to open the door, the Lord begins to fulfill His incredible promises.

We need to thank God every day that He is still sending His message of love and promise to the church. When you say, "Lord, I choose to respond to Your voice," He will lift you into His presence. It is a marvelous place to be!

FIVE

"It's Not Over!"

THE NEWSPAPER reporter asked, "Reverend Clement, what is a white man from South Africa going to tell the people of our country?"

I was in Perth, a city of over one million people in Western Australia.

Immediately I knew what the journalist meant. I said, "I am not here to represent South Africa. And I certainly won't be talking about apartheid or politics."

I felt like telling him what I had suffered because of standing with black people during my lifetime. But I was not there to vindicate myself or promote any causes.

"Then why did you come?" he asked.

"I am here to represent the kingdom of God. I have come to reach the unreachable and touch the untouchable."

The next day those words were on the front page of the newspaper. So were my picture and a story about the evangelistic crusade moving to a large auditorium.

About two weeks earlier I had come to Perth at the invitation of a local pastor. Just a handful of people attended the first service. But they were hungry for a word from God.

The Lord began to move in such an unusual way that people were coming from everywhere. There was such a wonderful outpouring of God's Spirit that within a few nights the building was jammed to capacity.

Several ministers in the area saw what God was doing and came to visit me. They said, "We believe we should turn this into a citywide campaign. Will you stay in Perth if we can arrange it?"

"Yes," I told them. "God is about to do something supernatural."

The Entertainment Center in Perth seats about six thousand, and they arranged to move the meetings there. "We can cordon it off to seat four thousand," one of the preachers said. "The last big evangelistic crusade we had drew about twenty-two hundred."

"I've got shocking news for you," I told them. "If God sends His word, the people will come. Open it up! We'll fill that place."

Someone Famous?

For two weeks — ever since I arrived in Perth — I had felt such a burden for Western Australia that I had entered a time of total fasting and prayer. I had not touched a scrap of food and had drunk only water. "Lord," I prayed, "send Your word. Send Your word."

The day we moved to the Entertainment Center the front page news story appeared. It said, "I have come to reach the unreachable and touch the untouchable."

Thousands and thousands of people poured into the arena until every seat was filled. The moment I walked onto the platform I could feel a special surge of God's power. It was like electricity. Even though I was weak from fasting, I felt ten feet tall.

While the large choir was singing, I prayed, "Lord, do something unusual tonight. We need to reach this city for You."

I was hoping that God would give me a prophetic word for some well-known person in the audience. "Bring someone who is famous into the kingdom," I prayed. "It will be such an example." I thought that perhaps a senator, an actor, a sports celebrity or a television reporter would be perfect. I wanted to see something so profound that people would go away saying, "Can you believe what happened tonight?"

I should have known that God doesn't speak because of my desires, but because of His sovereign will.

As the meeting proceeded, the choir sang "Amazing Grace," and I preached for about thirty minutes under a strong anointing. The power of the Lord so filled that auditorium that people were being saved, healed and baptized in the Spirit. But I continued to pray, "Lord, I know that You have a prophetic word for someone special here tonight. Show me the man or woman You are going to speak to."

As I was looking for direction from the Lord, I noticed a group of well-dressed people seated together, and I thought, *Surely it is one of them. Lord, do You have a special word I can give?* But nothing came.

Then I felt an urging in my spirit that said, "Look at the back of the auditorium. Do you see that seat at the end of the aisle in the last row? That's where I want you to go!"

I thought, *Have I heard the Lord correctly? Who would be so important that they would be sitting in the last row?*

As I walked through the huge auditorium I looked to my left and to my right for someone to whom the Lord would direct me to speak. But the only thing He said was, "I won't tell you anything until you go to the last seat in the last row."

People turned their heads and watched me intently as I continued to walk. They wondered whom I was going to call out. Whom was I going to prophesy over?

When I reached the back wall of the building, I saw the seat God had pointed out to me. Then, when I saw the person seated there, I thought, *This is impossible. Why would God have me speak to this person?*

In front of me was a disheveled teenager whose shirt was tattered and torn. I tried to disregard the odor of his body as I looked at his eyes. They were vacant and wounded with pain.

For a second I was frozen. Then God said to me, "Remember yourself! That's you!"

I suddenly saw myself as a wasted young man, high on heroin, stabbed and bleeding to death on a street in Port Elizabeth. And I remembered how someone came to my rescue and led me to the Savior. Those years of drugs, rock and rebellion had disappeared when the Lord penetrated my heart.

Now it was my turn to rescue someone else.

I called the young man by his name, and he recoiled like a frightened child. "Come with me," I said as I led him down the long aisle to the platform.

As we stood in front of that audience, I put my arms around him and said, "God says for me to tell you: 'This day I have become your Father.' "

The young man began to cry, and He asked Christ to come into his heart.

Bullets in the Barrel

I learned later that just three days before the meeting a dramatic story had been unfolding in the life of this six-teen-year-old boy. He had been in his hometown of Sydney, the largest city in Australia. Sydney was more than two thousand miles away from Perth. His father was an alcoholic and a hopeless drug addict. His mother had died because of a horrible beating — and his father had been accused of doing it.

The son, who was also on drugs, had come home one day and been severely beaten by his father. He had been literally kicked out of the door. He had broken bones, and he was bleeding. His father yelled, "I never want to see you again. Never! Never!" Then he said, "Today I disown you! I am not your father anymore!"

The young man took some of the last drugs he had, stumbled to the home of a friend and borrowed a gun. He had put some bullets into the barrel and said to himself, It's over! He was ready to take his own life. But instead, for no reason at all, he walked to the highway and began to hitchhike across Australia.

Three days later, still alone, he found himself sitting on the curb of a street in downtown Perth. He was still contemplating suicide.

Perth is a windy city, and suddenly a sheet of newspaper blew near him. He grabbed it. He was going to roll a "joint" and have a smoke.

As he was about to tear the paper, he saw the word *unreachable* on the page. Next to it was my picture.

The word seemed to jump right off the paper. *Unreachable,* he thought. *That's me!*

The scruffy, unkempt teen said to himself, *I need to get to this man if it's the last thing I do. Perhaps he has something to tell me.*

He looked back at the newspaper. The article said that I was going to be at the Entertainment Center. He glanced up and immediately saw the name of the building across the street: Entertainment Center. The doors were just opening for the first service.

He walked in and took a seat on the last row. As he waited for the service to begin, he thought, *I don't know if God knows me or cares about me. I don't know if Jesus exists, but I hope that God will do something for me.*

Now, standing on the platform, he was welcomed into the family of God.

The Christians in that city received him as one of their own. He was filled with the Spirit, grounded in the Word and began a ministry to young people on the streets of Perth.

The Lord knew who was the most important person in that service. We can always trust the sound of His voice.

Whom Does He Call?

Those who despised Christ and His followers scoffed whenever He talked with those who were despised. Do you remember what the Pharisees said when Jesus began speaking to a prostitute?

> A woman in the city who was a sinner, when she knew that Jesus sat at the table in the Pharisee's house, brought an alabaster flask of fragrant oil, and stood at His feet behind Him weeping; and she began to wash His feet with her tears, and wiped them with the hair of her head; and she kissed His feet and anointed them with the fragrant oil. Now when the Pharisee who had invited Him saw this, he spoke to himself, saying, "This man, if He were a prophet, would know who and what manner of woman this is who is touching Him, for she is a sinner" (Luke 7:37-39).

They did not understand that the Lord responds to faith, regardless of who the person might be. Jesus said, "I did not come to call the righteous, but sinners, to repentance" (Matt. 9:13). What did Christ tell the critical Pharisee?

"Therefore I say to you, her sins, which are many, are forgiven, for she loved much. But to whom little is forgiven, the same loves little."
And He said to her, "Your sins are forgiven" (Luke 7:47-48).

A gentleman in Florida recently asked me, "Does a person have to be righteous to receive the voice of the Lord?"
"Of course not," I replied. "Even though prophecy is primarily for the church, God has always used His voice to redeem humanity and to reveal His plans."
Jacob, the son of Isaac, was not exactly an honorable man. He was a liar and a deceiver. He tricked his brother out of his birthright for some bread and some lentil stew (Gen. 25:29-34). And Jacob even received his father's blessing by disguising himself as his brother (Gen. 27:1-41).
Nevertheless, God spoke to Jacob through a vision while he was sleeping on the ground with a stone for a pillow.

Then he dreamed, and behold, a ladder was set up on the earth, and its top reached to heaven; and there the angels of God were ascending and descending on it.
And behold, the Lord stood above it and said: "I am the Lord God of Abraham your father and the God of Isaac; the land on which you lie I will give to you and your descendants" (Gen. 28:12-13).

The Lord gave Jacob this promise:

Your descendants shall be as the dust of the earth; you shall spread abroad to the west and

89

the east, to the north and the south; and in you
and in your seed all the families of the earth shall
be blessed. Behold, I am with you and will keep
you wherever you go, and will bring you back to
this land; for I will not leave you until I have
done what I have spoken to you (vv. 14-15).

The man who lied and deceived was even given a brand-
new name. God said, "Your name shall not be called Jacob
anymore, but Israel shall be your name" (Gen. 35:10). And
he became the father of the twelve tribes of Israel.

Thoughts From Above

How does God accomplish His prophetic word? It begins
with just a thought. God thinks about something. And we
become in harmony with God — "tuned in" to His
thoughts. We begin to understand what He wants us to
know. " 'For I know the thoughts that I think toward you,'
says the Lord, 'thoughts of peace and not of evil, to give
you a future and a hope' " (Jer. 29:11).

There was person in the Bible who had a special understanding of the thoughts of the Lord. His name was David.

The confidence David established in his relationship
with the Lord was evident. His prayer to the Lord was
"Keep me as the apple of Your eye" (Ps. 17:8).

It was David who said, "How precious also are Your
thoughts to me, O God! How great is the sum of them! If I
should count them, they would be more in number than
the sand" (Ps. 139:17-18).

Have you ever wondered what God is thinking about
you?

When you are sick, do you think, *Does the Lord know the
pain I am feeling?* When your financial resources are low,
do you ask yourself if the Lord will ever shower His blessing on you?

It starts as a thought, then it becomes a word.

The Lord was speaking of His everlasting covenant to David when he said, "For My thoughts are not your thoughts, nor are your ways My ways" (Is. 55:8). This was not a statement of unbelief, but a plea from the heart of God. The Lord was saying, "I want My thoughts to become your thoughts. I want My ways to become your ways."

God says, "For as the heavens are higher than the earth, so are My ways higher than your ways, and My thoughts than your thoughts" (v. 9). He not only wants to lift the level of our listening, but desires that we know His mind.

If you could have just a glimpse of what God thinks about you, you would become a new person. His esteem for you is greater than you have for yourself.

Most people think God changes His mind about them because of their mistakes or failures. That may be how your friends and neighbors respond, but not the Lord. He created you in His image and sees the potential of your life.

Society teaches us to believe "three strikes, and you're out." But life is not a ball game with a rigid set of rules. And our alliance with God is not a legal contract, but a working relationship — a love covenant between you and your Creator.

What happens when a small child makes a mistake? Is the child banished from the family? No. And the Lord treats us the same way.

It is vital that we seek to know God's thoughts because they are the source of what He says. His mind becomes His voice. He declares:

> For as the rain comes down, and the snow
>   from heaven,
> And do not return there,
> But water the earth,
> And make it bring forth and bud,
> That it may give seed to the sower

And bread to the eater,
So shall My word be that goes forth from My
    mouth;
It shall not return to Me void,
But it shall accomplish what I please,
And it shall prosper in the thing for which I
    sent it (Is. 55:10-11).

God's words are *committed* words. When the Lord sends a word to you that says, for example, "Your child will come out of drugs," that is a commitment from the Lord on which He will never turn His back.

We need always to remember that the moment God says something to you, it is already a fact. And He gives you His pledge to uphold His part of the bargain.

God has made a commitment, but what about you? What is your part? If you believe that God *must* accomplish His prophetic word, you are mistaken. When the Lord begins to speak, it is your choice to accept it, believe it and act upon it. When God speaks, a door is opened for us. But we have to step through if we are to see the promise become a reality.

"We Are Waiting!"

Before Christ returned to heaven, He made a promise that God's voice would continue to speak to you and me. "And I will pray the Father, and He will give you another Helper, that He may abide with you forever...the Spirit of truth" (John 14:16-17).

Then Jesus said that when the Holy Spirit comes, "He will guide you into all truth; for He will not speak on His own authority, but whatever He hears He will speak; and He will tell you things to come" (John 16:13).

The prophetic word is part of the trinity. From the moment of creation, the voice of God has revealed the future.

When Christ was sent to earth, He also spoke about tomorrow. Now the Holy Spirit was about to descend. He would also speak of "things to come."

The Lord "commanded them not to depart from Jerusalem, but to wait for the Promise of the Father, 'which,' He said, 'you have heard from Me; for John truly baptized with water, but you shall be baptized with the Holy Spirit not many days from now' " (Acts 1:4-5).

When Christ had returned to heaven, 120 believers gathered in the upper room. They began waiting on God. I can imagine them praying, "Father, we know that Jesus was the Word, but You promised us something more. Lord, You said something about a Comforter. You said something about One who would be by our side. We are waiting! We are waiting!"

Then it happened! Scripture records:

> Suddenly there came a sound from heaven, as of a rushing mighty wind, and it filled the whole house where they were sitting. Then there appeared to them divided tongues, as of fire, and one sat upon each of them. And they were all filled with the Holy Spirit and began to speak with other tongues, as the Spirit gave them utterance (Acts 2:2-4).

There was not only a sound, there was *breath*. And they became the voice of God.

A Triple Restoration

As I learned at that meeting in Western Australia, we don't always understand why the Lord speaks as He does. But when the promise is ultimately revealed, we can see God's hand at work.

That was certainly true in the life of Simon Peter. Discovering how God dealt with him through prophecy is like finding the answer to how God speaks — and *why* He speaks.

So many people are like Peter. They have failed God miserably and feel ashamed to face Him. They hide themselves away and say, "Lord, I know I am never going to be used again because I have sinned." But if they will listen, God has a word of restoration.

Without question, Peter committed one of the most serious spiritual crimes possible. He denied the Lord Jesus Christ — not once, but three times.

Just before the crucifixion, while the high priest was questioning Jesus, Peter was waiting outside the courtyard.

> Then the servant girl who kept the door said to Peter, "You are not also one of this Man's disciples, are you?"
> He said, "I am not" (John 18:17).

A few minutes later, while he was warming himself by a fire, someone else asked Peter, "You are not also one of His disciples, are you?"

He denied it and said, "I am not!" (v. 25).

Then one of the servants of the high priest, a relative of him whose ear Peter cut off, said, "Did I not see you in the garden with Him?"

Peter then denied knowing Jesus again (vv. 26-27).

The story does not end with Peter being rejected by the Almighty. Far from it. After the resurrection of Christ, it is thrilling to see how God changes Peter's life. He had denied the Lord three times, but Christ offered him restoration three times.

Jesus appeared to His disciples at the shore of the Sea of Tiberias while they were fishing. When they came to the shore and all had breakfast together, Jesus said to Simon Peter:

"Simon, son of Jonah, do you love Me more than these?"

He said to Him, "Yes, Lord; You know that I love You."

He said to him, "Feed My lambs."

He said to him again a second time, "Simon, son of Jonah, do you love Me?"

He said to Him, "Yes, Lord; You know that I love You."

He said to him, "Tend My sheep."

He said to him the third time, "Simon, son of Jonah, do you love Me?" Peter was grieved because He said to him the third time, "Do you love Me?"

And he said to Him, "Lord, You know all things; You know that I love You."

Jesus said to him, "Feed My sheep" (John 21:15-17).

Before God revealed His plan for Peter's future, He dealt with the matter of restoration. And that is how He continues to speak to people today. He restores us, and then proclaims His promise.

It is tragic that when people sin, they believe they can never be restored. But if you are *willing* to be reconciled to Christ, He is waiting to receive you.

A Prophecy for Peter

After Simon Peter experienced God's forgiveness and was once again secure in Christ, God gave him a prophetic word. It was an unusual message.

Most assuredly, I say to you, when you were younger, you girded yourself and walked where you wished; but when you are old, you will

95

stretch out your hands, and another will gird you and carry you where you do not wish (John 21:18).

Those were words that Peter did not want to hear. He probably wondered what they meant. Was Christ talking about how he was going to die?

The first time I read those words I thought, *Is that really a significant prophecy? Where is the hope? Where is the promise?*

Peter may have interpreted the words to mean, "When I die, someone is going to dress me and carry me to the grave."

But Jesus was telling him something about tomorrow that was more positive and powerful than Peter could comprehend, as we will see.

So often we want to hear powerful words from God. I'm sure Peter would have liked Jesus to prophesy, "One day you are going preach in Jerusalem, and three thousand will be saved! You are going to pray for a crippled man at the temple gate, and he will be healed! You are going to lay your hands on people, and they will receive the Holy Spirit!"

What we must realize, however, is that *any* utterance that comes from the mouth of God has the power to release great miracles in our lives.

A Voice in the Prison

When Christ ascended to heaven, Peter began his ministry. The anointing he received in the upper room resulted in an unparalleled spread of the gospel. There were signs, wonders and miracles at every turn.

Peter became a new man. When he opened his mouth to speak, he had a new power. Thousands were added to the kingdom of God.

From that day until now Satan has been trying to stop that resurrection power. One of his initial attempts was to have Peter executed.

> Now about that time Herod the king stretched out his hand to harass some from the church. Then he killed James the brother of John with the sword. And because he saw that it pleased the Jews, he proceeded further to seize Peter also. Now it was during the Days of Unleavened Bread. So when he had apprehended him, he put him in prison, and delivered him to four squads of soldiers to keep him, intending to bring him before the people after Passover (Acts 12:1-4).

It is difficult to imagine what Peter was thinking when he knew James was beheaded by the soldiers. Would he be next? What would be the result of the mock trial that soon would take place? I'm sure he thought about the foreboding words of Herod: "I'm going to kill you after the Passover."

But while Peter was kept in prison, "constant prayer was offered to God for him by the church" (Acts 12:5).

The night before Herod was to bring him to trial, "Peter was sleeping, bound with two chains between two soldiers; and the guards before the door were keeping the prison" (v. 6).

How could Peter sleep in the face of such adversity? I believe that Peter went to prison filled with fear. But he began to pray, "God, reveal Your will to me. Please rescue me! Do You have a word I can cling to?"

While he was praying Peter may have said, "Lord, what did You tell me at the shore of the sea?" And he heard a still, small voice echo four words of Jesus: "When you are old!"

Perhaps he recalled the prophecy of Jesus and knew

there would be no execution. What had Jesus told him? "When you are old, you will stretch out your hands, and another will gird you and carry you where you do not wish" (John 21:18).

I believe Peter must have looked at himself and said, "I'm not an old man! I am still young! This is not my time to die!"

The words of Christ were not of death, but of hope and expectation. Suddenly the words of Christ flooded his spirit, and he entered God's peace. He fell asleep and waited for the deliverance of the Lord.

> Now behold, an angel of the Lord stood by him, and a light shone in the prison; and he struck Peter on the side and raised him up, saying, "Arise quickly!" And his chains fell off his hands (Acts 12:7).

Think of it! While Peter was waiting for his execution, he was sleeping so soundly that, even with a bright light shining, the angel had to strike him to wake him up. He was totally resting in the Lord's promise.

The words that were spoken next were an amazing fulfillment of Christ's prophecy.

> Then the angel said to him, "Gird yourself and tie on your sandals"; and so he did. And he said to him, "Put on your garment and follow me" (v. 8).

Why did the angel say "gird yourself"? Because Jesus had told Peter, "When you are old...another will gird you."

Why did the angel say "tie on your sandals" and "follow me"? Because Jesus told Peter that when he was old he wouldn't be able to walk by himself. The Lord said, "Another will...carry you."

This was not Peter's time to die! He was going to live. No

one else was going to dress him. He was still young and alive.

> And when Peter had come to himself, he said, "Now I know for certain that the Lord has sent His angel, and has delivered me from the hand of Herod and from all the expectation of the Jewish people" (v. 11).

Never take lightly the voice of the Lord. He gives you His word to use as a weapon against the powers of darkness that come against you. In the hour of your greatest battle you can cling to His promise and rest with great joy and confidence.

The time may come when you are in a prison of physical illness, bound by financial needs or, like the young man in Australia, abandoned and trapped by the pressures of life. But that is when you will hear the voice of God say, "It's not over! I have a great work for you to accomplish!"

SIX

THE GREAT
TRANSFORMATION

WHEN THE Lord rescued me from a self-destructive spiral of drugs and rebellion that left me dying in a gutter, I wanted to give Him my best. Everything about God's Word, Christian living and the church was new. All I could pray was, "Lord, all that I have is Yours. You have given me musical talent that I want to use for Your glory."

I waited and waited for God to reply. I was hoping that He would say, "I will greatly multiply your gift. Your songs will be used mightily to build the kingdom."

But instead the Lord said, "Kim, I am calling you to a prophetic ministry."

A prophet? I wondered. *Why would the Lord call me to be a prophet?*

But the Lord had spoken. What I later learned was that when God speaks, He creates something from nothing — something that was not there before. Why does He operate in such a manner? I believe it is so we cannot take the glory or credit for His manifestation. It is important that the world be compelled to say, "That is God, not man."

Three important things happen when God speaks:

1. He creates.

2. He forms.

3. He transforms.

And something more. God vindicates His transformation by giving us His oil of anointing.

There is nothing to compare with God's "creative word." He does not speak something into your life that you already have; He creates something that you don't already possess.

The way God causes that to happen, however, is quite unusual. Many people believe that the Lord always creates a finished product immediately. But one meaning for the word *create* in the Bible is to "fashion something" — to "prepare" it for habitation.

I like to think of God's prophetic words as an outer shell that He allows to be filled and completed. For example, being born again and becoming a new creation in Christ are only the beginning of what we will become. God first creates something, then He inhabits it.

Every time God speaks to you — whether it is through an individual or during a time of meditation and prayer — His creation is at work. You can *feel* it. It's like a burst of energy that explodes within your spirit. Suddenly, you possess something you did not have before. And that is just the start.

Squeezing and Fashioning

Immediately after God speaks something into creation, He takes the second step: He *forms*. First God *said*, "Let Us make man" (Gen. 1:26). He "created man in His own image" (v. 27). How did God do it? By forming him.

> And the Lord God formed man of the dust of the ground, and breathed into his nostrils the breath of life; and man became a living being (Gen. 2:7).

Most people are in a big hurry. "Lord, I need to hear from You right now," they pray. But when God speaks, we don't always see the final product instantly. After He creates us, He begins the process of squeezing each contour and fashioning each profile. And all the time He is watching our response.

I once was asked, "If God created every person, why do some turn out to be saints and others sinners? Why are some parents loving and kind, while others are cruel and abusive?"

Why *do* some people become liars, murderers and thieves? They reach that state by rebelling against God's attempts to form them. As free moral agents, they *choose* the path they travel.

Between creation and formation the Lord gives us the option to either accept or reject His redemptive plan. Your refusal of salvation allows Satan to take your carnal clay and fashion it into something evil.

When the Bible says that we are "to be conformed to the image of His Son" (Rom. 8:29), it means that we are to be fashioned or shaped into the Lord's likeness.

We serve an imaginative God. When He speaks, He creates something totally distinctive and fresh. It is almost impossible to comprehend that there are more than five billion people on the earth, yet no two people have identical fingerprints.

In my travels I am constantly amazed by the people I meet. Every personality is distinct — each with its own disposition, nature and temperament. And in all these people is a constant flow of fresh creativity. How exciting it is that each person has a spiritual personality that is being formed into the image of Christ.

When God calls people to His service, He gives them a unique ministry. But some people find that difficult to understand. Many young evangelists have stood before mirrors and tried to look and sound like Billy Graham or Oral Roberts. They wanted to imitate every vocal inflection and every gesture. But God has not called you to be someone else. He has called you to be you!

> But now, thus says the Lord, who created you,
>   O Jacob,
> And He who formed you, O Israel:
> "Fear not, for I have redeemed you;
> I have called you by your name; you are Mine"
>   (Is. 43:1).

We all have our own personalities and our own names. But into whose image does God want to shape us? *His* image.

Paul, writing to the church at Galatia, described spiritual formation as being like a woman giving birth to a child. It is accompanied by travail, anguish and suffering. But that is nothing compared with what is brought into the world through the pain — the baby!

> It is good to be zealous in a good thing always, and not only when I am present with you. My little children, for whom I labor in birth again until Christ is formed in you... (Gal. 4:18-19).

Always remember — we first become a new creation, then we are formed.

The Breath of Life

What happens next is even more inspiring. After God creates us and forms us, He *transforms* us.

Do you remember what happened after God formed man? He "breathed into his nostrils the breath of life" (Gen. 2:7) and transformed Adam into a living being.

Today that important work is accomplished through the Holy Spirit. The Spirit is also imparted by the breath of the Lord. Just after the resurrection, Jesus gathered His disciples together and said:

> "Peace to you! As the Father has sent Me, I also send you." And when He had said this, He breathed on them, and said to them, "Receive the Holy Spirit" (John 20:21-22).

As millions of people can testify, that same power is still available.

It is the transforming power of the Spirit that makes it possible for us to be in the presence of the Lord. On the Mount of Transfiguration, Christ was changed from one state of existence to another. Scripture records that "the appearance of His face was altered, and His robe became white and glistening" (Luke 9:29).

Centuries before, God's presence was so mighty on Moses "that the children of Israel could not look steadily at the face of Moses because of the glory of his countenance" (2 Cor. 3:7).

When he came down from Mount Sinai to deliver the Covenant, "the skin of Moses' face shone, then Moses would put the veil on his face" (Ex. 34:35).

But now the covenant is "written not with ink but by the

Spirit of the living God, not on tablets of stone but on tablets of flesh, that is, of the heart" (2 Cor. 3:3). Because of the change that happens inside, we become transformed so that we are able to look directly into the face of the Lord. It is possible because "when one turns to the Lord, the veil is taken away" (2 Cor. 3:16).

Through the power of the Spirit "we all, with unveiled face, beholding as in a mirror the glory of the Lord, are being transformed into the same image from glory to glory, just as by the Spirit of the Lord" (2 Cor. 3:18).

You may ask, "Do I have to wait until I get to heaven to be transformed?"

No. It happens now.

> Therefore, if anyone is in Christ, he is a new creation; old things have passed away; behold, all things have become new (2 Cor. 5:17).

In our natural state we cannot become the voice of God to the world. We might have the best education and speak eloquently, but our effect will be meaningless. It is only when we are changed by the Spirit that we can minister healing and deliverance in the name of the Lord. That's what gives us authority over Satan and the ability to touch the untouchable.

The Lord forms us by dealing with our spirits and our souls. But when we are transformed, it allows the formation that has taken place to be expressed outwardly. It is something that comes from the inside out.

When the glory of God descended on Christ, the outward manifestation of what had taken place inside was His face being altered and His robe glistening white.

A Metamorphosis

More than once I have seen sincere people attempt to

operate in the realm of the Spirit without first being transformed. They have read enough Scripture to know what is available, but they have never allowed the Lord to "breathe" on them. The results are tragic. When carnal people receive the word of a carnal personality, they leave exactly as they came — empty, dissatisfied and frustrated.

Within the church are people who have a good "stage" appearance and can totally captivate an audience. The services they lead may be highly entertaining, but where are the results? Two months after their visit, ask those who attended, "What can you remember about the meeting? Did anything happen that had a lasting impact on your life?"

"Well, no," they may reply, "but he was a good speaker."

Talent must never be confused with a transformed life. We need to heed the words of Paul.

> I beseech you therefore, brethren, by the mercies of God, that you present your bodies a living sacrifice, holy, acceptable to God, which is your reasonable service. And do not be conformed to this world, but be transformed by the renewing of your mind, that you may prove [show forth, express] what is that good and acceptable and perfect will of God (Rom. 12:1-2).

There is a big difference between being conformed and being transformed. In the world of science, a total transformation is called a metamorphosis. That is what happens when a fuzzy caterpillar sheds its skin and becomes a butterfly, or when a tadpole comes out of the water and turns into a frog.

Throughout the New Testament we are warned against being formed into the mold of this world. Paul tells us that the transformation that should take place includes a new source of knowledge.

106

> Now we have received, not the spirit of the
> world, but the Spirit who is from God, that we
> might know the things that have been freely
> given to us by God (1 Cor. 2:12).

Who is our teacher?

> These things we also speak, not in words which
> man's wisdom teaches but which the Holy Spirit
> teaches, comparing spiritual things with spiritual.
> But the natural man does not receive the things
> of the Spirit of God, for they are foolishness to
> him; nor can he know them, because they are
> spiritually discerned. But he who is spiritual
> judges all things, yet he himself is rightly judged
> by no one (vv. 13-15).

It is only natural for people to say, "I could never be
transformed by the renewing of my mind." And that is true
— of our old minds.

As Paul concluded, "For 'who has known the mind of the
Lord that he may instruct Him?' But we have the mind of
Christ." (v. 16).

Every day we need to claim God's promise that the Spirit
will illuminate our thought lives. We need to pray that
knowledge of the Word will transform us — that there will
be an outward expression of what is taking place within.

How can we demonstrate the mind of Christ? By express-
ing His utterance instead of our own feelings.

We can only "prove" the perfect will of God when we
have been reconstructed by the Lord. That's how we can
know perfect love, perfect joy and perfect peace. It does
not come from our own strength, but from His.

> Every good gift and every perfect gift is from
> above, and comes down from the Father of lights,

107

with whom there is no variation or shadow of turning (James 1:17).

It is through this glorious process that we are allowed to take on the properties and nature of the Almighty.

There are some who teach that we are "little gods" on earth. But that thinking is filled with danger and can lead to a self-centered, humanistic theology. We are not gods, but we become *like* God through redemption provided by Christ. For example, we cannot make decisions on behalf of God.

You and I are God's representatives on the earth. We are His arms, His legs and His feet, and we can become the voice of God. We are not God, but He has chosen to share His heavenly heritage with us.

Nine Gifts, Nine Fruits

As a manifestation of our spiritual transformation, the Lord allows us to receive and "operate" in one or more of the gifts of the Spirit. We know they come from above because they are beyond our natural abilities — and they are not our permanent possessions. Most importantly, these gifts are not for our personal benefit, but "for the profit of all" (1 Cor. 12:7).

Nine gifts of the Spirit are listed in 1 Corinthians 12:8-10:

1. Word of wisdom

2. Word of knowledge

3. Faith

4. Gifts of healings

5. Working of miracles

6. Prophecy

7. Discerning of spirits

8. Different kinds of tongues

9. Interpretation of tongues

These are not to be earned, but are gifts — freely provided by God. But He also offers us the fruit of the Spirit. What is the difference? *Gifts are given, but fruit grows.*

Just as there are nine gifts, there are also nine fruits of the Spirit. According to Galatians 5:22-23, they include:

1. Love

2. Joy

3. Peace

4. Longsuffering

5. Kindness

6. Goodness

7. Faithfulness

8. Gentleness

9. Self-control

As you are being formed by God, the fruit continues to grow. But the metamorphosis takes place when the gifts of the Spirit start operating, and you begin to manifest what is happening within. You'll find that one is linked to the other. Each gift and each fruit will cause the expression of the other to become beautiful and perfect.

If someone gives a word of knowledge or prophecy without love or joy, the gift is out of balance. That is why it is important that the fruit be allowed to mature and develop before the gifts are exercised.

What is the result of being transformed? You become

able to express the true nature of God. The Lord will not permit you to represent Him unless this spiritual change has taken place. Otherwise, you would be an impostor or a misrepresentative.

It would be wonderful to say that every person who speaks in the name of the Lord has been transformed by the power of God. Unfortunately, that is not the case. That is why Christ gave this warning: "Beware of false prophets, who come to you in sheep's clothing, but inwardly they are ravenous wolves" (Matt. 7:15).

What is the test of a true representative of the Lord? Jesus said, "You will know them by their fruits...every good tree bears good fruit, but a bad tree bears bad fruit" (vv. 16-17).

Then He added:

> Not everyone who says to Me, "Lord, Lord," shall enter the kingdom of heaven, but he who does the will of My Father in heaven. Many will say to Me in that day, "Lord, Lord, have we not prophesied in Your name, cast out demons in Your name, and done many wonders in Your name?" And then I will declare to them, "I never knew you; depart from Me, you who practice lawlessness!" (Matt. 7:21-23).

We are not being asked to develop a suspicious spirit or to blindly accept everything said in the name of the Lord. Instead, we should be looking for the evidence of a transformed life. Is the fruit of the Spirit evident? Is the will of God being expressed, or the opinions of men?

You may wonder why so few people enter that spiritual dimension. I believe it is because of stubbornness and selfish desires. By yielding to their carnal nature, they never reach their potential in Christ. It is also true that the Lord will not change us against our will.

God has priorities for those who would become His

voice. First, He requires that our foundation be built totally on Him. The apostle Paul wrote:

> As you have therefore received Christ Jesus the Lord, so walk in Him, rooted and built up in Him and established in the faith, as you have been taught, abounding in it with thanksgiving (Col. 2:6-7).

Then he warned:

> Beware lest anyone cheat you through philosophy and empty deceit, according to the tradition of men, according to the basic principles of the world, and not according to Christ. For in Him dwells all the fullness of the Godhead bodily; and you are complete in Him, who is the head of all principality and power (vv. 8-10).

Our relationship to the Lord is vital. Many people who are busy ministering *for* God do not understand the necessity of ministering *to* God.

At the church of Antioch, just before the disciples anointed Saul and Barnabas by the laying on of hands, "they ministered to the Lord and fasted" (Acts 13:2). Then they received direction from the Holy Spirit.

The Spirit of Balaam

During a recent crusade I told the people, "Don't let anyone who is not anointed pray for you or prophesy over you." To be anointed means to have the approval of God.

After the service a man questioned me about that statement, saying, "Isn't that a little hard? What about someone who is sincere and means well? What harm can be caused?" Then he asked, "And how can we always know if someone is truly anointed?"

They were legitimate questions. In far too many instances God has been blamed for something that He had no part in. Just because someone says "Here is what God told me to tell you" or "Thus saith the Lord" does not mean that God has truly spoken.

After Jesus explained to His disciples that He was going to be crucified, Peter stopped Him and said, "Far be it from You, Lord; this shall not happen to You!" (Matt. 16:22). But the Lord rebuked him for being the mouthpiece of the devil and said, "Get behind Me, Satan! You are an offense to Me, for you are not mindful of the things of God, but the things of men" (v. 23).

The voice of the Lord and kingdom principles are serious matters. We are not discussing a man-made theory, but a spiritual transformation.

I have not been one to receive a great number of dreams and visions from the Lord, but over a period of several months, I had the same dream night after night. I saw prophets coming to the church in great numbers. They would stand before the people and tell them incredible things about themselves. In my dream I would say, "Lord, this man is so accurate." But God would say, "He is a false prophet."

I could not understand the dream. "Why are You showing me this?" I asked God.

He replied, "Because demonic powers have unleashed the spirit of Balaam upon the church."

I recalled the story. Balaam loved unrighteousness. But God sent a donkey speaking with a man's voice to restrain his madness (2 Pet. 2:15-16).

The dream made me realize that the problems God addressed in Old Testament times remain to this day.

Is it possible that an imitation can replace the genuine? If you have never tasted the real thing, the artificial seems perfectly normal — you might even think it is better.

I was amazed at what happened when one pastor visited me in South Africa. He came from a country that had no fresh-squeezed orange juice. When I gave him a glass of the real thing, he actually tried to spit out the first mouthful. "I've never tasted anything like that before," he said.

To him, the imitation was better because he was accustomed to it. He had never experienced the authentic. We finally convinced him how great fresh orange juice is.

That's the way it is with the anointing. The imitation will be perfectly acceptable to a person who has never experienced a genuine move of the Spirit.

Quality Spices

We can understand more about the anointing by looking at God's specific instructions to Moses for preparing the anointing oil. To me, the ingredients symbolize the standard by which we can measure the anointing today.

> The Lord spoke to Moses, saying: "Also take for yourself quality spices — five hundred shekels of liquid myrrh, half as much sweet-smelling cinnamon (two hundred and fifty shekels), two hundred and fifty shekels of sweet-smelling cane, five hundred shekels of cassia, according to the shekel of the sanctuary, and a hin of olive oil. And you shall make from these a holy anointing oil, an ointment compounded according to the art of the perfumer. It shall be a holy anointing oil" (Ex. 30:22-25).

In the generations that have passed since Moses, people continue to seek God's anointing. It is a sign of God's approval on their lives. Sometimes they receive it while they are praying. At other times they receive it while they

113

are worshipping the Lord through music or praise.

Four primary "quality" spices were brought together to produce the anointing oil. I think they point to characteristics that must be present before people can express what God is trying to do through them.

1. Myrrh

The first ingredient Moses was asked to find was five hundred shekels (approximately twelve and a half pounds) of liquid myrrh.

Myrrh is a spice that is fragrant to smell but bitter to taste. It speaks to me of *love and suffering*.

Those who live under the anointing of the Lord know what it means to suffer for righteousness' sake. They are misunderstood, lied about and often ridiculed. Yet the Lord expects them to suffer in love.

To taste such love — to suffer — is bitter, but once you have gone through it, God provides a fragrance that is unequaled.

2. Cinnamon

Next he was to add two hundred and fifty shekels (a little over six pounds) of sweet-smelling cinnamon.

Cinnamon speaks to me of "glowing and burning" because of the fiery flavor of this spice. So it reminds me of *holy jealousy for the honor and glory of God*. When someone says something to mock or belittle the Savior, I can feel myself burning inside as I come to His defense.

Persons under the anointing of the Lord will glow with a fire that comes from within. You will recognize that fire when you are in their presence.

3. Cane

God instructed Moses to add two hundred and fifty shekels of sweet-smelling cane to the mixture.

A sugarcane plant produces sturdy stalks up to fifteen

feet tall that stand erect and grow best in miry, soggy soil. As applied to the anointing, sugarcane refers to *standing upright in the midst of sin and perversion.*

Before the sweetness can be extracted from the sugarcane, it must be crushed. If there is no brokenness, there can be no fragrance. Those whom God uses as His voice are people who have a broken and contrite spirit. They are the ones who stand tall in His kingdom.

4. Cassia

The final spice to be added was five hundred shekels of cassia. *Strong's Concordance* notes that the Hebrew root word for cassia is *qadad,* which means "to stoop." Stooping is a depiction of *worship and sacrifice.*

So cassia reminds me that God's anointing does not come to those who refuse to bow their knee in worship or who fail to make a full surrender of their life to the Lord.

The Essential Element

After Moses poured in these four ingredients, God instructed him to add olive oil — the element that would blend them all together. We must let the oil of the Holy Spirit blend together these important characteristics in our lives. As Peter said of Christ:

> God anointed Jesus of Nazareth with the Holy Spirit and with power, who went about doing good and healing all who were oppressed by the devil, for God was with Him (Acts 10:38).

The very word *messiah* means "anointed one."

Why are the ingredients of the anointing oil so important? Because the oil is made fragrant by the spices, just as the Holy Spirit is enhanced by these characteristics in our lives.

You may have all the necessary spices (characteristics), but without the Holy Spirit combining them — leading and directing you — you are never going to have that special fragrance.

Many people never experience the transforming power of the Lord or His anointing because they lack an element required by the Lord. They have love, but do not know suffering. Or they have worship, but refuse to sacrifice.

God told Moses to mix the ingredients into "a holy anointing oil, an ointment compounded according to the art of the perfumer" (Ex. 30:25). The Lord is the Perfumer who takes everything we are going to become and gently compounds it together.

When the anointing oil was prepared, the Lord told Moses to anoint those who would serve Him as priests and to instruct the people that "this shall be a holy anointing oil to Me throughout your generations" (v. 31).

Then the Lord gave three specific commands concerning the use of the sacred oil:

1. "It shall not be poured on man's flesh" (v. 32). To put it another way, we are not to anoint a man of flesh or one who is unregenerated.

2. "Nor shall you make any other like it, according to its composition" (v. 32). The formula was to be valued and used only for the intended purpose. It was not to be imitated.

3. "Whoever compounds any like it, or whoever puts any of it on an outsider, shall be cut off from his people" (v. 33). The "outsider" is someone who is not one of God's people. We cannot give what is sacred to a noncovenant person.

As we will see, God's message to the children of Israel remains His warning to you and me. He is saying, "Don't become careless with what is sacred."

The same God who created, formed and transformed you is protective of what has been accomplished. He wants nothing to interfere with the anointing He has prepared for you.

SEVEN

DIVINITY OR DIVINATION?

THROUGHOUT HISTORY man has longed to become divine.

In ancient Rome, Caesar Augustus, Nero and other emperors declared themselves to be divine, and people likened them unto gods. The same was true of rulers in ancient Greece.

For centuries the monarchs of England, France and Germany said their power derived from "the divine right of kings" — that their right to rule came directly from God. Accordingly, it was up to the Almighty, not the subjects, to punish a wicked king.

The desire to be superhuman is also seen in athletics. World-class competitors will do almost anything in their quest for greatness. They crave to be heralded as the strongest or the swiftest.

Canadian track star Ben Johnson wanted to become the "world's fastest man" at the Seoul Olympics in 1988. He was so obsessed by his goal that he resorted to taking drugs to enhance his speed. As a result, his dreams were dashed, and he was stripped of his titles.

What the world seeks through earthly means can be ours through being children of the living God. We have been given the ability to become partakers of the divine. He allows us to receive the essence of His godliness, personality and character.

As I will describe in the rest of this chapter, God has chosen to share with us a divine nature, divine power and a divine inheritance.

A New Nature

Peter, who was an eyewitness to the transfiguration of Christ, explains how it is possible for us to participate in the very nature of God. He was not writing to the unbeliever, but "to those who have obtained like precious faith with us by the righteousness of our God and Savior Jesus Christ" (2 Pet. 1:1).

Peter said,

> His divine power has given to us all things that pertain to life and godliness, through the knowledge of Him who called us by glory and virtue, by which have been given to us exceedingly great and precious promises, that through these you may be *partakers of the divine nature*, having escaped the corruption that is in the world through lust (2 Pet. 1:3-4, italics added).

The voice of God is a voice of promise, and this is one of God's greatest commitments: We are to become "partakers of the divine."

Becoming a partaker means that we share in something

119

but do not totally possess it. In other words, we are only partaking in that substance called divinity. We are a participant in His divine expression on this Earth. Because of this unique union, the Lord can minister to us, speak through us and allow us to become His representatives.

In your daily routine of driving to work, dealing with business matters or raising a family, you may say, "I certainly don't feel divine."

Well, you are not! You are only a *partaker* of the divine. But God can express His heavenly nature through you whenever He pleases — on a bus, in a car or at home. Suddenly He comes upon you, and the divine is expressed as you utter the will of God in a specific situation.

We are not puppets walking through the earth without purpose. His will is accomplished through our affinity with Him. The attributes, the properties and the nature of God are allowed to flow through us. It is part of our heritage as children of God.

Because of the work of Christ on the cross, we have a divine nature.

Sorcery in Samaria

When the world sees the power of God operating in the lives of believers, it is only natural for them to covet the same blessing. They become so envious that they attempt to imitate the divine. That is what happened in Samaria.

A genuine revival was taking place in the city through the ministry of Philip.

> The multitudes with one accord heeded the things spoken by Philip, hearing and seeing the miracles which he did. For unclean spirits, crying with a loud voice, came out of many who were possessed; and many who were paralyzed and lame were healed (Acts 8:6-7).

But another man in the city had enjoyed the respect of the people before Philip came.

> There was a certain man called Simon, who previously practiced sorcery in the city and astonished the people of Samaria, claiming that he was someone great, to whom they all gave heed, from the least to the greatest, saying, "This man is the great power of God." And they heeded him because he had astonished them with his sorceries for a long time (vv. 9-11).

Because Simon astounded them with his evil supernatural powers, they actually heralded him as being "the great power of God."

We need to be cautious of people — even inside the church — who astonish us with their exploits. Astonishment is not enough. We need to observe their lives and determine that they have truly been transformed. We must see conviction, repentance, love and unity.

When people have never experienced the power of the Lord, they will call almost anything divine. The disciples themselves knew how it felt to have people elevate them to a position far higher than the Lord intended (see Acts 14:8-18; 28:1-6).

For years the people had treated Simon as someone divine. The Bible says they "heeded" his words. Then the gospel was preached in Samaria with authority, anointing and power. Scripture records that "when they believed Philip as he preached the things concerning the kingdom of God and the name of Jesus Christ, both men and women were baptized" (Acts 8:12).

What a difference the name of Jesus makes! People were coming to Christ in great numbers. But what about Simon? How did he respond?

> Then Simon himself also believed; and when he was baptized he continued with Philip, and was amazed, seeing the miracles and signs which were done (v. 13).

The sorcerer was saved! He became a friend to Philip and observed firsthand the healing and deliverance that was taking place. That's why he was on hand when the believers first received the Holy Spirit.

> Now when the apostles who were at Jerusalem heard that Samaria had received the word of God, they sent Peter and John to them, who, when they had come down, prayed for them that they might receive the Holy Spirit. For as yet He had fallen upon none of them. They had only been baptized in the name of the Lord Jesus. Then they laid hands on them, and they received the Holy Spirit (vv. 14-17).

For the first time since Christ ascended to heaven, God's glory was being transferred from one human person to another. Peter and John were sent by the church at Jerusalem to see what was happening in Samaria. They began laying hands on people to receive the Spirit.

In the Old Testament, laying on of hands was used to confer blessing (Gen. 48:13-20), to transfer guilt from the sinner to the sacrifice (Lev. 1:4) and to commission someone for a God-ordained responsibility. Moses brought Joshua before the priest, "And he laid his hands on him and inaugurated him, just as the Lord commanded" (Num. 27:23).

When Christ came to the earth, He continued the practice.

Jesus brought healing to the leper as He "put out His hand and touched him, and said to him, 'I am willing; be cleansed' " (Mark 1:41). He gathered children around Him, "put His hands on them, and blessed them" (Mark 10:16).

After the Lord returned to heaven, the apostles commissioned other believers — including Philip — to conduct church business. And "when they had prayed, they laid hands on them" (Acts 6:6).

What Peter and John were imparting was more than a blessing. They were transferring the very power of God through the Holy Spirit. It was a power that Simon had never seen before, and immediately he wanted that same ability. But he was totally ignorant regarding how God chose to deliver the Spirit. He thought the gift could be purchased.

> Now when Simon saw that through the laying on of the apostles' hands the Holy Spirit was given, he offered them money, saying, "Give me this power also, that anyone on whom I lay hands may receive the Holy Spirit" (Acts 8:18-19).

Simon had been saved and baptized but had much to learn about spiritual gifts. He did not understand that the power of God is not for sale. He probably thought that his sorcery brought him great esteem, fame and fortune. If he gave these men a substantial sum of money, perhaps they would give this new power to him.

The price Peter and John paid for the anointing, however, was much different. The authority that rested on them came through prayer, fasting, suffering and travail — along with love, joy and worship.

But like so many people who want to display the divine, Simon wanted easy access and instant results. He wanted to take control of the power of God and offered payment for the privilege.

Many might be tempted by material gain. But not Peter. He said to Simon, "Your money perish with you, because you thought that the gift of God could be purchased with money!" (v. 20).

I believe Peter spoke those words because he recalled God's warning to Moses which we discussed in the previous chapter (Ex. 30:31-33). If the Lord's oil of anointing is given to someone who is not spiritually ready to receive it, the one who imparts it "shall be cut off from his people" (v. 33).

Simon probably had heard about what had happened to Ananias and Sapphira. They perished when Peter exposed them for lying to the Holy Spirit about an offering they had given to the apostles (Acts 5:1-11).

Now Peter was giving a similar warning to Simon. Because the new convert thought he could purchase the power of the Spirit, Peter told him, "Your money perish with you." Then he added, "You have neither part nor portion in this matter, for your heart is not right in the sight of God. Repent therefore of this your wickedness, and pray God if perhaps the thought of your heart may be forgiven you" (Acts 8:21-22).

Peter did not promise forgiveness. He asked Simon to repent and to pray that the Lord "perhaps" might pardon his transgression. The disciple told him, "I see that you are poisoned by bitterness and bound by iniquity" (v. 23).

Then Simon answered and said, "Pray to the Lord for me, that none of the things which you have spoken may come upon me" (v. 24).

Just because a person believes on Christ does not automatically qualify him to receive everything that is divine. The transference that takes place by the laying on of hands is sacred. It must never be given to someone who is not right before God.

"Psychic Hotline"

For every supernatural gift that comes from God, Satan

has created a substitute. Ancient diviners foretold events by countless methods — from observing the inner parts of slaughtered sheep or goats to examining the patterns of drops of oil falling into a cup of water. Persons called *oracles* interpreted these so-called messages from the gods.

There have been many attempts to stamp out satanic worship and witchcraft — some of them misguided. In the 1600s suspected witches were tied up and thrown into the water. Those who sank were considered innocent. Those who floated were considered to be witches — and were burned at the stake or hanged.

It seems nothing has changed. Palm-reader and fortune-teller signs dot the landscape of the nation. Thousands of people are involved in dream interpretation, necromancy (communicating with the spirits of the dead), tarot card reading, voodoo and astrology.

Former First Lady Nancy Reagan made headlines when it was learned that she consulted an astrologer in San Francisco to determine what days her husband should not fly in an airplane. Members of England's royal family have traveled to India to meet with gurus.

It is shocking to turn on a television set and see a famous Hollywood celebrity promoting a "psychic hotline." For two dollars a minute you can make a phone call and hear a tape recording that will supposedly reveal your future. The number should be 1-900-666-6666.

Why are people calling? Because mankind is crying out for a revelation from above — regardless of what kind of a god it is from.

When you listen to sorcerers, fortune-tellers and astrologers, you are only hearing Satan's plan for your life. It may sound enticing, but it will lead you down a path of destruction. Remember the fortune-teller who told me that I would become famous for my music? That wasn't God's plan. It was Satan's. The path toward becoming a famous musician nearly killed me.

Those who read God's Word and hear His voice, however, are receiving the message of a loving God. They learn who they are in Christ and what they can become in His kingdom.

Because you are redeemed, you have the right to go to Him and ask Him anything at anytime. For example, you may ask, Lord, what do You have planned for my little child? And He may choose to show you what He has prepared for your boy or girl — and even their children. Then, when Satan attempts to divert their paths, you can stand against him and say, "No. That's not the purpose of God for them. Devil, I defy you!" And you can break Satan's power in their lives.

Fraudulent Faith

What is divination? It is simply an imitation of the divine. Moses told the children of Israel:

> There shall not be found among you anyone who makes his son or his daughter pass through the fire, or one who practices witchcraft, or a soothsayer, or one who interprets omens, or a sorcerer, or one who conjures spells, or a medium, or a spiritist, or one who calls up the dead (Deut. 18:10-11).

Then he added:

> For all who do these things are an abomination to the Lord (v. 12).

Under the influence of Satan, people are lured into consulting the powers of darkness. This evil is put on the same level as rebellion against God. According to Scripture, it leads to death.

Saul, the first king of Israel, "died for his unfaithfulness which he had committed against the Lord, because he did not keep the word of the Lord, and also because he consulted a medium for guidance" (1 Chron. 10:13).

It is Satan's aim to substitute the influence of evil spirits for the authority of the voice of God.

Divine Power

When Paul and Silas brought the message of Christ to Philippi, Satan decided to disturb their efforts.

> Now it happened, as we went to prayer, that a certain slave girl possessed with a spirit of divination met us, who brought her masters much profit by fortune-telling. This girl followed Paul and us, and cried out, saying, "These men are the servants of the Most High God, who proclaim to us the way of salvation" (Acts 16:16-17).

Many people believe that when Satan speaks, it will either be a lie or a direct confrontation. They think it will be easy to say, "Oh, that is the devil talking. Shut up and sit down."

But Satan is much more subtle and sly. He knows that "death and life are in the power of the tongue" (Prov. 18:21), and he wants to deceive you with flattery.

In this case he used flattery and a spirit of exhibitionism in his attempt to control or manipulate the work of the Lord.

Some observers must have thought the girl was promoting the apostles when again and again she said, "These men are the servants of the Most High God, who proclaim to us the way of salvation." Were her words accurate? Yes. Did God say it? No. That was the difference.

Satan is in the business of harassment and torment.

And this she did for many days. But Paul, greatly annoyed, turned and said to the spirit, "I command you in the name of Jesus Christ to come out of her." And he came out that very hour (Acts 16:18).

Why did Paul stop her? He realized that the words spoken by this young woman would cause great damage to the church that was being established.

Accuracy does not guarantee that a person is truly a man or woman of God. The Lord may get your attention through a prophet who tells you where you live. But never forget that Satan knows your name and address, too. The slave girl at Philippi was imitating the divine, and it turned to divination.

We should also beware of flattery and adulation. We love to hear someone say, "You are special in the sight of God." But I would much rather have a prophet tell me about an area of my life God wants me to correct or improve than be flattered. It is truth that will set us free.

The prophet Micah in the Old Testament warned against those who expound for personal gain.

> Thus says the Lord concerning the prophets
> Who make my people stray;
> Who chant "Peace"
> While they chew with their teeth,
> But who prepare war against him
> Who puts nothing into their mouths:
> Therefore you shall have night without vision,
> And you shall have darkness without divination;
> The sun shall go down on the prophets,
> And the day shall be dark for them (Mic. 3:5-6).

It is tragic when men and women of the Lord no longer hear what the Spirit is saying but remember what the Spirit said in the past. They have no fresh revelation. Instead, in their desperate attempt to appeal to the masses, they imitate the anointing and fall into the trap of divination.

To hear an "old" word is like eating manna that has been left outside. It is spoiled and stinks (Ex. 16:20). Here is what Micah said would happen because Israel no longer heard the voice of the Lord:

> The seers shall be ashamed,
> And the diviners abashed;
> Indeed they shall all cover their lips;
> For there is no answer from God (Mic. 3:7).

Why would they be ashamed and abashed? Because

> Her priests teach for pay,
> And her prophets divine for money.
> Yet they lean on the Lord, and say,
> "Is not the Lord among us?
> No harm can come upon us" (v. 11).

The result was destruction.

> Therefore because of you Zion shall be plowed
>   like a field,
> Jerusalem shall become heaps of ruins
> And the mountain of the temple
> Like the bare hills of the forest (v. 12).

The Bible calls divination an abomination. God told the children of Israel that "the person who turns after mediums and familiar spirits, to prostitute himself with them, I will set My face against that person and cut him off from his people" (Lev. 20:6).

Three Questions

Not every prophet is a true spokesman for God. During a great drought in Israel, Jeremiah said to the Lord:

> Behold, the prophets say to them, "You shall not see the sword, nor shall you have famine, but I will give you assured peace in this place" (Jer. 14:13).

But the Lord responded:

> The prophets prophesy lies in My name. I have not sent them, commanded them, nor spoken to them; they prophesy to you a false vision, divination, a worthless thing, and the deceit of their heart...By sword and famine those prophets shall be consumed! (vv. 14-15).

How can you tell if someone is a genuine prophet of the Lord? You should ask three questions.

1. Is the prophecy coming out of the prophet's own mind, or is it from God?

2. Is the prophet speaking out of his or her own spirit, or the Lord's?

3. Has the prophet actually seen something that comes from God?

Those three issues were addressed by Ezekiel when the Lord told him:

> Son of man, prophesy against the prophets of Israel who prophesy, and say to those who prophesy out of their own heart, "Hear the word

130

of the Lord!" Thus says the Lord God: "Woe to the foolish prophets, who follow their own spirit and have seen nothing!" (Ezek. 13:2-3).

Someone involved in divination sees nothing and counterfeits the divine. The Lord said,

> O Israel, your prophets are like foxes in the deserts...They have envisioned futility and false divination, saying, "Thus says the Lord!" But the Lord has not sent them; yet they hope that the word may be confirmed (vv. 4,6).

And here are the consequences of divination.

> "Because you have spoken nonsense and envisioned lies, therefore I am indeed against you," says the Lord God. "My hand will be against the prophets who envision futility and who divine lies; they shall not be in the assembly of My people, nor be written in the record of the house of Israel, nor shall they enter into the land of Israel" (vv. 8-9).

It is vital that you know who is speaking into your life — whether it is God or Satan. The devil can be communicating with you in ways that you may not recognize. He may flatter you.

Sudden Darkness

Saul and Barnabas traveled to Cyprus, and

> when they had gone through the island to Paphos, they found a certain sorcerer, a false prophet, a Jew whose name was Bar-Jesus, who

was with the proconsul, Sergius Paulus, an intelligent man. This man called for Barnabas and Saul and sought to hear the word of God (Acts 13:6-7).

Satan knows where to attach himself. The proconsul was the Roman governor of the island.

But Elymas the sorcerer (for so his name is translated) withstood them [Barnabas and Saul], seeking to turn the proconsul away from the faith (v. 8).

But it didn't work.

Then Saul, who also is called Paul, filled with the Holy Spirit, looked intently at him and said, "O full of all deceit and all fraud, you son of the devil, you enemy of all righteousness, will you not cease perverting the straight ways of the Lord? And now, indeed, the hand of the Lord is upon you, and you shall be blind, not seeing the sun for a time."
And immediately a dark mist fell on him, and he went around seeking someone to lead him by the hand (vv. 9-11).

What was the political leader's response? "Then the proconsul believed" (v. 12). The proconsul saw the judgment of God coming.

If we expect to see God's righteousness in the governments of the world, we need to have the boldness of Paul and express the utterance of God. He became the mouthpiece of the Lord on the earth.

Satan could not give Paul the power to pronounce judgment over Elymas the sorcerer. Only God has that power.

132

And He spoke the word through one of His servants. Paul did not come as a teacher, but he gave the greatest illustrated lecture any man could give.

I recently heard a religious leader say, "We don't need signs and wonders. The Word is sufficient." The proconsul would not have believed if that manifestation had not taken place. It was a sign of authority. And God has given us that same capability — not to speak the word of blindness, but to be obedient to the voice of God so we can dispel the power of divination.

Every day I pray for a display of God's power upon the earth. We have experienced the Jesus movement and the charismatic movement. Now I believe it is time for the unveiling of God's kingdom on the earth.

I believe it will come through people like you and me who are committed to becoming His voice. But first we must realize that we have His divinity inside of us. People will ask, Where is the kingdom? We can answer in the words of Jesus, "For indeed, the kingdom of God is within you" (Luke 17:21).

Out of the Fire

The Lord makes it possible to access His power at the time of our greatest need.

Paul said that he escaped from a shipwreck and swam to the shore of the island of Malta.

> The natives showed us unusual kindness; for they kindled a fire and made us all welcome, because of the rain that was falling and because of the cold. But when Paul had gathered a bundle of sticks and laid them on the fire, a viper came out because of the heat, and fastened on his hand (Acts 28:2-3).

As the people gathered around the apostle and "saw the creature hanging from his hand, they said to one another, 'No doubt this man is a murderer, whom, though he has escaped the sea, yet justice does not allow to live' " (v. 4).

But Paul had divine power. "He shook off the creature into the fire and suffered no harm" (v. 5).

The people hardly knew how to respond.

> They were expecting that he would swell up or suddenly fall down dead; but after they had looked for a long time and saw no harm come to him, they changed their minds and said that he was a god (v. 6).

Again, it is human nature for unbelievers to deify people who have power from God. It's an instinctive reaction.

For the next three days one of the leading citizens of the island, Publius, opened his home to Paul.

> And it happened that the father of Publius lay sick of a fever and dysentery. Paul went in to him and prayed, and he laid his hands on him and healed him. So when this was done, the rest of those on the island who had diseases also came and were healed (vv. 8-9).

As Paul departed, the people honored him in "many ways" and "provided such things as were necessary" (v. 10).

No power on earth is able to overcome the children of the Lord. When we confront the powers of darkness, the Lord is there to shine His eternal light and confound our foes. Listen to His words:

> I am the Lord, who makes all things,
> Who stretches out the heavens all alone,

134

Who spreads abroad the earth by Myself;
Who frustrates the signs of the babblers,
And drives diviners mad (Is. 44:24-25).

A Divine Inheritance

Not only has God given us a divine nature and power,
He has given us a divine inheritance. Paul reminded the
Ephesians of this:

> In Him you also trusted, after you heard the word
> of truth, the gospel of your salvation; in whom
> also, having believed, you were sealed with the
> Holy Spirit of promise, who is the guarantee of
> our *inheritance* until the redemption of the pur-
> chased possession, to the praise of His glory
> (Eph. 1:13-14, italics added).

He also prayed that the Ephesians would know "what is
the hope of His calling, what are the riches of the glory of
His *inheritance* in the saints" (Eph 1:18, italics added).

Today when you pray, thank the Lord that inside your
spirit dwells the divine nature of God, the divine power of
God and the divine inheritance of God.

EIGHT

WHO IS
SPEAKING?

L ATE ONE night I was praying after experiencing a serious back problem that did not improve. The Lord said to me, "You have been defiled by divination."

When those words came to me, I was shocked because I did not believe that as a man of God I could be defiled by somebody else. I said, "Lord, what do you mean 'defiled by divination'?"

I knew that people could injure themselves by adulterous thoughts, lies, anger, pride and lust. Scripture tells us:

> Do not love the world or the things in the world.
> If anyone loves the world, the love of the Father
> is not in him. For all that is in the world — the
> lust of the flesh, the lust of the eyes, and the

pride of life — is not of the Father but is of the world (1 John 2:15-16).

"Lord, I have tried to overcome these things. How else can Satan attack me?"

"He can do it through the power of words," answered the Lord.

As I opened the pages of Scripture, the Spirit showed me how people suffer when a satanic force, "a familiar spirit," speaks into their lives.

> For the idols speak delusion;
> The diviners envision lies,
> And tell false dreams;
> They comfort in vain.
> Therefore the people wend their way like
>   sheep;
> They are in trouble because there is no shep-
>   herd (Zech. 10:2).

> "Behold, I am against those who prophesy false dreams," says the Lord, "and tell them, and cause My people to err by their lies and by their reck-lessness. Yet I did not send them or command them; therefore they shall not profit this people at all," says the Lord (Jer. 23:32).

Moses warned the people of Israel of the danger of divination.

> Give no regard to mediums and familiar spirits;
> do not seek after them, to be defiled by them: I
> am the Lord your God (Lev. 19:31).

The word *defiled* comes from a Hebrew word which means "to be foul, especially in a ceremonial or moral sense; to be contaminated." It's a very strong word, often used to indicate sexual immorality or idol worship.

Moses was warning the people that words of prophecy which are not from the Lord are as dangerous as idol worship and sexual sin.

Spoken by a Stranger

We need to be extremely careful about accepting what people say. The faith teaching that Christians have heard in recent years says that we are to make a positive confession, and we should. But we need to remember that other people's words can affect us as well.

For example, if someone speaks in prophecy to you and you detect a spirit of anger — beware. I am not saying you need to know the intimate details of that person's life. What you discern in the person's spirit is the only warning you need.

Even before such a person says, "This is what God is instructing me to tell you," be careful. You should not, however, become skeptical of *everyone* who stands on the platform. In most cases you can trust the fact that your spiritual leaders — your "shepherds" — have been wise in screening and selecting those who will minister to you.

The potential for danger is greatest with those who come to you on a personal basis. They are the ones who corner you after a meeting or outside of the church with a "special word from God" for you. I call them "pew prophets" or "parking lot prophets." When you don't know about the personal life of such a person, you risk receiving a "familiar spirit" that is not from the Almighty.

We are not referring to someone who calls on the phone to say "Let's go fishing" or "Let's go shopping." Nor am I saying that a prophet is only valid if he or she has a well-known ministry. But we must use discernment with anyone who declares, "Thus says the Lord." We must be concerned with anyone who attempts to persuade you to do something that is contrary to what God has spoken to you.

Defilement takes place when words of dishonor are placed in your spirit — words that are proclaimed as being straight from God, but they are far from it. What is spoken can cause serious harm to your family, your business and your spiritual life.

The Danger of Defilement

Something that is defiled is unclean, impure or filthy. Satan knows that the church is to be without "spot or wrinkle or any such thing, but that it should be holy and without blemish" (Eph. 5:27). The enemy never sleeps in his attempt to tarnish the church through the power of deceitful words spoken from the mouths of false prophets.

If the person who attempts to prophesy over you has not been sent from God, then who has given him or her the word? A "familiar spirit" has. The real danger, then, is that you will be defiled — or contaminated — by whatever that person harbors in his or her life. It is sad to see people attempt to use the gifts of the Spirit without the approval or anointing of God.

The Bible lists three major causes of defilement.

1. *You can be defiled by a spirit of bitterness.*
The author of Hebrews wrote:

> Pursue peace with all men, and holiness, without which no one will see the Lord: looking diligently lest anyone fall short of the grace of God; lest any root of bitterness springing up cause trouble, and by this many become *defiled* (Heb. 12:14-15, italics added).

2. *You can be defiled by disobedience.*

In his letter to Titus, Paul said, "To the pure all things are pure, but to those who are *defiled* and unbelieving nothing is pure; but even their mind and conscience are *defiled.* They profess to know God, but in works they deny Him, being abominable, disobedient, and disqualified for every good work" (Titus 1:15-16, italics added).

God equates a person who is defiled with an unbeliever who may claim to know the Lord but whose actions — as a result of disobedience — will cause that person to be disqualified for service.

3. *You can be defiled by the tongue.*

The spoken word has the power to desecrate the entire body.

> Even so the tongue is a little member and boasts great things. See how great a forest a little fire kindles! And the tongue is a fire, a world of iniquity. The tongue is so set among our members that it *defiles* the whole body, and sets on fire the course of nature; and it is set on fire by hell (James 3:5-6, italics added).

Always be aware "lest Satan should take advantage of us; for we are not ignorant of his devices" (2 Cor. 2:11).

When the Lord told me I had been defiled by divination, I was lying on my back, unable to walk. I had been to the hospital twice for surgery, and I finally cried out to God, "What is happening?"

God answered, "This is what happened: You were defiled by divination."

"When?"

"The day those people at the convention spoke over you."

I remembered the day. I was attending a convention, and

a group of people who were self-proclaimed prophets gathered around me and prophesied. They were complete strangers to me.

I had never heard so many good words in my whole life. They prophesied that I was going to go to Cairo to speak to princes and sheiks in their tents. I think Queen Elizabeth even got in there somewhere. I was going to have houses in this country and houses in that country. I would be rich and have clothes and all of that.

When they finished speaking, I said to myself, *I'll just put that word aside on a little shelf in my heart.*

The Lord told me in the hospital, "Those people did not hear or see anything from Me. That was not My word. Therefore, you were defiled."

What I should have done was reject those messages immediately. When I finally broke the power of that defilement, we had complete freedom in our home, and my health was restored.

Can We Know?

How can we defend against defilement? By being sensitive to the spirit of a person's heart. Jesus said, "For out of the abundance of the heart the mouth speaks" (Matt. 12:34). In some cases words are spoken from the *lack* of abundance of the heart.

The most important thing is not what a person says, but the condition of his innermost being. One of the gifts God has made available for us is the "discerning of spirits" (1 Cor. 12:10). It is a gift that should be operating through you.

More than once, when I have felt God's warning signs, I have stopped a person who was attempting to speak into my life. Otherwise I would have been defiled.

On the other hand, it is easy to use the wrong measuring stick to judge people. They may have personalities that do not please you. Their exteriors may be angry or calm. Their voices may be loud or soft. But that is not what counts. The only question you need to ask is, What about their heart?

It is not necessary to live with a spirit of distrust. You don't have to act as God's detective, telling people, "Don't speak to me." The Lord expects us to use a loving spirit, offering gentleness and consideration in dealing with others.

After years of being involved in a prophetic ministry, I can tell instinctively whether or not a person has a heart that is yielded to the Lord. It is a spiritual perception that God allows all of us to develop.

Some people say, "I will wait to see what the person says or how he or she acts." But you may be misguided since everyone has faults and failures.

You may say, Oh, I would never allow Sister Smith or Brother Jones to pray over me. I've seen too many shortcomings in their lives. Any child of God can make a mistake. That does not disqualify that person in the sight of God. The Lord only rejects someone whose heart has become impure.

The words people speak spring from the heart to the tongue and then become the spoken word. We can look past the vocabulary, the grammar, the culture and the accent. What flows from a person's heart is what truly affects us.

At a recent conference I spoke with a married couple who said, "Pray for us. We are having tremendous problems in our home and with our personal health." They said, "We just don't understand it. We have fasted and prayed. And we have fought Satan."

Suddenly the Spirit of the Lord gave me a word for them. I felt lead to say, "Tell me about something that was spoken over your life about two years ago." After they reflected on my question, they told me the time, the place and the person who had spoken a prophetic word to them. Ever since that moment, everything in their life had gone downhill.

"Where is that person now?" I wanted to know.

"Well, he is no longer in the ministry. In fact, I don't believe he is living for the Lord," the husband responded.

Defilement was brought to this couple through a person whose heart was not right. We rebuked that word over their lives, and they were set free. There was a wonderful turnaround in their lives.

You Are the Tabernacle

God revealed Himself to the people of Israel at Mount Sinai. Later in the Old Testament we read that "the Lord dwells in Zion" (Joel 3:21). The move from Sinai to Zion served to change the Israelites from one dimension of law to another. There was greater freedom in their praise and worship, but it was still legalistic.

In Zion (or Jerusalem), God's earthly presence was concentrated in one specific place — a tent. David "prepared a place for the ark of God, and pitched a tent for it" (1 Chron. 15:1).

When Christ came to earth and was crucified for sin, God allowed man to enter a new dimension. Now the Lord no longer dwells in an ark, a tent or a physical tabernacle that is thousands of miles away from us. We don't have to travel to the Holy Land to find God. He resides in you and me. We are His dwelling place. And that is the joy of the new covenant.

We have been given the right "to enter the Holiest by the blood of Jesus, by a new and living way which He consecrated for us" (Heb. 10:19-20) The Bible says we are now the house (Heb. 3:6), the tabernacle and the temple.

Scripture declares:

For you are the temple of the living God. As God has said:

I will dwell in them
And walk among them.
I will be their God,
And they shall be My people (2 Cor.
6:16).

Because of what Christ made possible, we have a great responsibility. In Old Testament times the priests were accountable for what entered the sanctuary. But now *we* are the sanctuary and are answerable for what enters *our* lives.

As Christians, our bodies are no longer our possessions. They have been bought with a price and are the temples of almighty God. When you fully understand the sacred trust the Lord has placed in your care, you will protect and cherish your body with your very life. You will not allow anything that does not belong to enter the door of the sanctuary.

The Lord is so jealous of this habitation that He will judge anyone who defiles it — whether it is you or someone else.

Do you not know that you are the temple of God and that the Spirit of God dwells in you? If anyone defiles the temple of God, God will destroy him. For the temple of God is holy, which temple you are (1 Cor. 3:16-17).

The tabernacle God has given you is not made by hands. It is a gift from on high.

Your body is the temple of the Holy Spirit who is in you, whom you have from God, and you are not your own (1 Cor. 6:19).

The Lord's desire is to place a wall of protection around us to prepare us for the great day that is coming.

One way Satan attempts to defile us is to plant seeds of doubt. For example, I spend countless hours each year flying across oceans in jumbo jets. The devil always tries to whisper in my ear, "Did you read about the plane that crashed in Scotland?" or "Kim, I don't mean to disturb you, but have you heard about the terrible weather up ahead?"

I reject Satan's words because I know that my life is in God's hands, not his. Instead, I claim the Scripture that declares: "Being confident of this very thing, that He who has begun a good work in you will complete it until the day of Jesus Christ" (Phil. 1:6) As a result, I am at peace in the midst of any storm that may develop.

Once, when Jesus was crossing the Sea of Galilee with His disciples, a great windstorm arose.

> The waves beat into the boat, so that it was already filling. But He was in the stern, asleep on a pillow. And they awoke Him and said to Him, "Teacher, do You not care that we are perishing?"
>
> Then He arose and rebuked the wind, and said to the sea, "Peace, be still!" And the wind ceased and there was a great calm. But He said to them, "Why are you so fearful? How is it that you have no faith?" (Mark 4:37-40).

When you are in God's perfect will, you have no reason to be afraid. Your own will can fall victim to the devil's intimidation and control, but you can't be swayed when you're in the will of God. Remember, Christ gave Himself for our sins "that He might deliver us from this present evil age, according to the will of our God and Father" (Gal. 1:4). Why would He do that? Because it is only when you are out of God's will that Satan can destroy you.

And the evil one wants to snatch you from the Father's

will. He may attempt to do it by giving you a word through a false prophet to lead you in the wrong direction.

The Two Temples

There are two types of temples spoken about in the New Testament. The Greek word *hieron* is used to describe the entire temple structure including the outer court — the physical building that is the house of God. But the word *naos* is used to describe the inner sanctuary of the temple which only priests could enter. Metaphorically, *naos* refers to the inner sanctuary of our hearts. It says in 1 Corinthians 6:19, "Do you not know that your body is a temple [naos] of the Holy Spirit, who is in you?" (NIV).

When Jesus went to the temple at Jerusalem, He was appalled to find people selling cattle, sheep and doves — even exchanging money in such a holy place. Scripture records His response.

> When He had made a whip of cords, He drove them all out of the temple, with the sheep and the oxen, and poured out the changers' money and overturned the tables (John 2:15).

The temple He entered was the *hieron* — the building made of stone and mortar. He said "Take these things away! Do not make My Father's house a house of merchandise!" (v. 16).

The Pharisees challenged the Lord and asked, "What sign do You show to us, since You do these things?"

Jesus answered, "Destroy this temple, and in three days I will raise it up" (vv. 18-19).

They did not understand that the *naos* Jesus referred to was not the physical building in which they were standing. The Jews then said:

146

"It has taken forty-six years to build this temple, and will You raise it up in three days?"

But He was speaking of the temple of His body (vv. 20-21).

Jesus was trying to tell them, "I am the inner sanctuary of the Father. I am the glory of God. If you destroy this glory, in three days it will be raised up."

They had no idea that the Lord's words would be fulfilled by His crucifixion and resurrection.

We are not Christ on the earth, but His majesty resides in our temple of flesh and blood. That is why God told Paul to instruct the people to guard the temple against defilement. We are the glory of the Lord and His sanctuary on earth.

Nothing we have done has made us worthy vessels for God's habitation. Instead, it is the work of Christ that allows God to say, "Because of the blood of My Son, you are now My glory."

The Lord looks beyond a sacred tent, an ark of the covenant or a temple of gold and precious stones. What pleases Him is the brilliance of a heart that is pure and clean.

Foreigners Not Allowed!

Since we are the temple of the Lord, we need to observe the principles found in the temple ordinances. Ezekiel talked a great deal about our responsibilities in this. The Lord brought Ezekiel to the temple and told him:

> Son of man, mark well, see with your eyes and hear with your ears, all that I say to you concerning all the ordinances of the house of the Lord and all its laws. Mark well who may enter the house and all who go out from the sanctuary (Ezek. 44:5).

147

God was saying, "Pay close attention to those who would enter your temple — the dwelling place of the Most High." The Lord gave this commandment because each time someone speaks into your life, he or she is entering your sanctuary. If someone is not qualified to enter, turn that person away.

God's word to Ezekiel was:

> Say to the rebellious, to the house of Israel, "Thus says the Lord God: 'O house of Israel, let us have no more of all your abominations. When you brought in foreigners, uncircumcised in heart and uncircumcised in flesh, to be in My sanctuary to defile it — My house — and when you offered My food, the fat and the blood, then they broke My covenant because of all your abominations' " (vv. 6-7).

The people were guilty of allowing "foreigners" — those whose hearts were not right with God — to enter the sanctuary and defile it.

Some immediate signs of not being in covenant with the Lord are having no horizontal covenantal relationship and no "covering" — no one to whom to be accountable. People who operate like this have independent ministries without the oversight of local churches. The Bible speaks of this type of person as "uncircumcised."

God is looking for people who are in covenant with the Word, with ministry leadership, with His church and with Him. When we have made a pact with the Lord, we should be ready to become open before both God and man.

The Lord said through Ezekiel:

> "You have not kept charge of My holy things, but you have set others to keep charge of My sanctuary for you." Thus says the Lord God: "No for-

eigner, uncircumcised in heart or uncircumcised in flesh, shall enter My sanctuary, including any foreigner who is among the children of Israel" (vv. 8-9).

Centuries later, Paul told the church at Ephesus the good news that, as Christians, we are no longer from an alien country.

Now, therefore, you are no longer strangers and foreigners, but fellow citizens with the saints and members of the household of God, having been built on the foundation of the apostles and prophets, Jesus Christ Himself being the chief cornerstone, in whom the whole building, being joined together, grows into a holy temple in the Lord (Eph. 2:19-21).

The "you" to which Paul referred is plural. We are being built together into a holy habitation. And God is bringing His people together now. As citizens of heaven, we have rights and privileges that cannot be measured. It is something foreigners will never know.

A unique safety is yours when you are under spiritual authority. Many times people have called me and asked, "Will you please come to my church?" I am flattered by their invitations and have often responded, "I'd love to come."

As I place the receiver back on the phone, I sometimes sense a check in my spirit. When that happens I immediately call Fred Roberts at my home church in South Africa, or I call another minister I respect and say, "This pastor has asked me to come. What do you feel about it?"

When there is agreement, I go. Scripture declares that "where there is no counsel, the people fall; but in the multitude of counselors there is safety" (Prov. 11:14).

There is protection when you operate in covenant with someone else.

Who Can Speak?

You may be saying, "I understand that I am not allowed to have a foreigner enter my sanctuary. But who *is* allowed to speak into my life?"

Ezekiel allowed three categories of people to enter the temple.

> But the priests, the Levites, the sons of Zadok, who kept charge of My sanctuary when the children of Israel went astray from Me...They shall enter My sanctuary, and they shall come near My table to minister to Me, and they shall keep My charge (Ezek. 44:15-16).

A *priest* is someone who is set apart and consecrated to be engaged in holy matters. God tells us not to allow someone who is not anointed by the Lord to speak over our lives.

For every prophet called by God, Satan will raise up an impostor. The devil will do everything in his power to send an immoral mouthpiece your direction. That is why we need to be in constant prayer to discern the difference.

The second group God appoints as keepers of the sanctuary are the *Levites*. The sons of Levi were given to God for His exclusive sacred use (Num. 8:9-14). The word *Levite* is derived from a Hebrew root word that means "to join." The Lord is looking for people who are joined both to God and to their fellow man.

The third category of people allowed in the sanctuary were *the sons of Zadok*. The name *Zadok* comes from a Hebrew root word that means "righteousness." Therefore, the sons of Zadok were the sons of righteousness.

When deciding who should be speaking over your life, you would be wise to apply the same test.

1. Are they anointed by God? And do they have delegated authority from God?

2. Are they in a covenant relationship with other people of God?

3. Are they righteous? Do they prove to be people of integrity by lives that are accountable?

Unfortunately, it is rare for people to pause and reflect on a prophetic word they are receiving. They see someone operating in the gifts of the Spirit and are in awe of what is happening. Then they quickly call their friends and exclaim, "You should hear the amazing things this person is saying." They give practically no attention to the issues of anointing, righteousness and commitment to the Lord.

Jesus said that you can identify false prophets "by their fruits" (Matt 7:16).

> And Aaron cast down his rod before Pharaoh and before his servants, and it became a serpent. But Pharaoh also called the wise men and the sorcerers; so the magicians of Egypt, they also did in like manner with their enchantments (Ex. 7:10-11).

Through trickery, the king's wizards imitated God's miracle. But the Lord had the final word. Do you recall what happened to the sorcerers' snakes? The Bible says that Aaron's snake swallowed all of their snakes (v. 12).

Often the results of a prophetic word cannot be determined when the seed is planted, but when the harvest comes. It is only natural to get excited when God's Spirit moves in a meeting. But I continue to tell people, "Don't judge my ministry by what happens in a particular service. Call me in two or three months — or even in one year." After some time passes, then we can really know what took place as a result of hearing God's voice.

A Great Day Coming

The Lord tells us that those who will reign with Him are people whose garments have not been defiled (Rev. 3:3-4). What is the reward for the overcomer? "He...shall be clothed in white garments, and I will not blot out his name from the Book of Life; but I will confess his name before My Father and before His angels" (v. 5).

We are fast approaching the hour that has been described as the conflict of the ages. Without question we are going to see the things of the Lord being duplicated by false apostles, false teachers and false prophets as never before.

At the same time we will see a victorious outburst of God's expression on the earth — and you and I will participate in it. Truth will swallow up evil. The power of God will be unprecedented, and we will be ushered into a land that knows no defilement.

We will also hear the voice of God as He says, "Well done."

NINE

IF YOU
ONLY KNEW!

DURING A service in Rhode Island I noticed a young man in the audience with his arms crossed, and he was frowning. I could tell that he was suffering from a disease that affected his face.

I felt led to walk over to him because God was directing me to those who were unsaved. He was a handsome young man despite his obvious health problems. When I asked him to stand, he rose reluctantly. I could see that he was extremely weak.

Then God gave me a prophetic word concerning some specific things about his life.

I said, "Sir, opportunity stands at your door. You have a choice. The Lord says, 'If you will turn to Me I will raise you up, heal your bones and make you a man of God. You will live to tell the world of My glory and power.' "

That message clearly surprised the young man.

I spoke with some of his relatives after the meeting. I learned that he was dying of a rare type of bone cancer and had only months to live. His relatives had convinced him to travel all the way from California to attend the meeting. I also was told that he was a rebellious young man who wanted little to do with Jesus or the church. All of his past religious experiences had been disappointing.

An evangelist would have given an altar call for him. A person with the gift of healing would have laid hands on him for an instant miracle. But I was there to deliver a prophetic word from the Lord. Each of the fivefold ministries is unique.

The young man did not receive salvation during that meeting. I had given him the word of the Lord. Now it was up to him to accept or reject God's call to repent.

No Preconditions

When Jesus told His disciples to perform miracles in His name, He didn't say, "Ask them if they are believers. Find out if they speak in unknown tongues. See if they know the doctrines of the church."

Jesus simply said, "Heal the sick, cleanse the lepers, raise the dead, cast out demons. Freely you have received, freely give" (Matt. 10:8). He told the disciples, "Heal the sick who are there, and say to them, 'The kingdom of God has come near to you' " (Luke 10:9). There were no preconditions to Christ's healing power. In fact, I believe God allows miracles to happen so people will be called to repentance.

Jesus did not say the kingdom of God would be *upon* them. He said it was *near* them. When the anointing of the Lord is present, it offers the opportunity for someone to enter the kingdom.

When that young man in Rhode Island sat down, he was not suddenly free of cancer. But he left that meeting with a new idea about who Jesus was. He realized that, even in his pathetic state, God was concerned enough to speak to him.

The Bible says, "See that you do not refuse Him who speaks. For if they did not escape who refused Him who spoke on earth, much more shall we not escape if we turn away from Him who speaks from heaven" (Heb. 12:25).

The next day the young man told his sister, "I want Jesus. I need this Christ the man was preaching about."

"Let's pray together," she said. As the two of them prayed, he surrendered his heart to the Lord.

That night he attended the service once again, now a transformed young man. The scowl was gone. He was lifting his hands and celebrating his salvation — and he had been physically healed as well.

What Do You Expect?

You only have to read a few pages of the Bible to know that God's ways are never dull and boring. He rarely accomplishes His purpose through repetition. Instead, His commandments and promises are always fresh.

In fact, His ways are so unique that some people do not even know the Lord is speaking to them. That's how it was when Jesus spoke to the woman at the well.

As far as she was concerned, the man conversing with her was a total stranger. She said, " 'How is it that You, being a Jew, ask a drink from me, a Samaritan woman?' For Jews have no dealings with Samaritans" (John 4:9).

Jesus answered her, "If you knew the gift of God, and who it is who says to you, 'Give Me a drink,' you would have asked Him, and He would have given you living water" (v. 10).

The Lord was encouraging the woman to ask questions,

saying, in effect, "If you only knew what was available, you would begin to ask, and the Father would begin to give." If she had only known it was Jesus, she could have had "living water."

When I stand before people to minister in the name of the Lord, I feel like pleading with them: "If you only knew the gift that God has for you!" or "If you only knew that the Lord is speaking to you!"

If people could just comprehend, they would ask and receive. They would seek and find. They would knock, and the door would be opened. We need to absorb as much knowledge as possible concerning what the Lord has in His storehouse — whether it is about healing, wisdom, prophecy or the other gifts of the Spirit.

The Muddy River

Would you settle for something you expect to hear rather than let the Lord give you something you thought was impossible? His word may not be what you imagine. He may not even address the issue that's facing you at the moment.

That's what happened to Naaman, the commander of the Syrian army, a mighty man of valour — and a leper. A young girl from Israel who was a servant to Naaman's wife had said, "If only my master were with the prophet who is in Samaria! For he would heal him of his leprosy" (2 Kin. 5:3).

So Naaman went to the king of Israel, who told him how to get to the prophet Elisha's house.

> Then Naaman went with his horses and chariot, and he stood at the door of the house of Elisha. And Elisha sent a messenger to him, saying, "Go and wash in the Jordan seven times, and your flesh shall be restored to you, and you shall be clean" (vv. 9-10).

That is not what Naaman imagined he would hear. When this proud pagan reached the home of the prophet, he believed he knew exactly how this man would perform the miracle. He had the scenario scripted perfectly. When his expectations weren't met, Naaman became furious and went away, saying:

> Indeed, I said to myself, "He will surely come out to me, and stand and call on the name of the Lord his God, and wave his hand over the place, and heal the leprosy" (v. 11).

He became even more incensed at the thought of washing in the muddy Jordan river. So he turned and went away in a rage. His servants encouraged Naaman to try what Elisha had commanded. When he did, "his flesh was restored like the flesh of a little child, and he was clean" (v. 14).

The instruction given by Elisha demonstrated to Naaman that his healing would not come from the purity of the water, but from the power of the God of Israel. But he received only because he obeyed the prophet.

He ran back to Elisha and said, "Indeed, now I know that there is no God in all the earth, except in Israel" (v. 15).

That's the creative God we serve.

Why does the Lord give instructions as specific as those He gave to Naaman? God told Naaman exactly where he should go because that place — the muddy Jordan River — became God's habitation at that point in time. If someone else had leprosy, went to the same river and dipped seventy or even *seven hundred* times, that person would not be healed.

You can't expect to live on the prophetic word given to someone else. The Lord gives unique, specific words. It is a private matter between you and God that cannot be reproduced.

Many people do not receive the promise of the Lord for the same reason the world did not receive Jesus when He walked on the earth. Christ was the Living Word, but He did not conform to their expectations and guidelines.

They expected Him to follow Old Testament customs and behave in a strict, well-defined manner. They were shocked that a person who claimed to be the Son of God would not follow their regulations. But by refusing Jesus, they also rejected the Word. Two thousand years have passed, and the problem remains. When the voice of the Lord speaks, most people fail to listen because of their preconceived notions of how God should respond. Then, when God gives them an answer they don't want to hear, they immediately close their minds and hearts.

I am reminded of what happened after a service I conducted. The pastor took me aside and said, "Kim, that is not what our people expected to hear."

"I'm sorry you feel that way," I responded, "but the Lord doesn't give us what we want to hear, but what we need."

Time for Action

The Lord is able to speak miracles into your life, but don't presume that He will always act alone. He will probably demand action on your part.

In Jerusalem during the time of Christ, a pool called Bethesda was located by the Sheep Gate. Every day it attracted "a great multitude of sick people, blind, lame, paralyzed, waiting for the moving of the water" (John 5:3).

They believed that an angel came to the pool at certain times and stirred up the water. Then whoever stepped in the pool first was made whole.

> Now a certain man was there who had an infirmity thirty-eight years. When Jesus saw him lying there, and knew that he already had been in that

condition a long time, He said to him, "Do you want to be made well?" (vv. 5-6).

Why did the Lord ask the man such an obvious question? Of course he wanted to be healed! Christ knew both the man's physical ailment and the condition of his heart. But He wanted to see the man respond to his need — to take the initiative that would result in his healing.

> The sick man answered, "Sir, I have no man to put me into the pool when the water is stirred up; but while I am coming, another steps down before me" (v. 7).

For thirty-eight years he waited for someone else to come and help him. He was saying, "I have no one to do it for me." He didn't realize that the miracle was not in the water, but in responding to the voice of the Lord.

> Jesus said to him, "Rise, take up your bed and walk." And immediately the man was made well, took up his bed, and walked (vv. 8-9).

The Lord wants us to be in divine communication with Him. Once that happens, we can expect Him to intercede on our behalf.

Our relationship must be directly with the Father, not through a second or third party. We just need to say, "Lord, I'm in an impossible situation. Tell me what to do." Nothing compares with specific direction from the Lord.

What was the lesson the Lord taught at the pool of Bethesda? Don't expect God to move unless you take the first step yourself.

In most instances, Christ's miracles were accompanied by a command to do something specific. He often healed people through His sovereign touch or through His spoken word, but most of the time He would also give them a directive, such as "rise up," "walk" or "wash your eyes."

Here is how Jesus asked people to put their faith into action.

- To the man with the withered hand at the synagogue, Jesus said, "Stretch out your hand" (Matt. 12:13). When he stretched it out, it was restored as whole as the other.

- When Jesus came to the ten lepers in Samaria, He told them, "Go, show yourselves to the priests" (Luke 17:14). As they were on their way to the priests, they were cleansed.

- To the nobleman whose son was close to death, He said, "Go your way; your son lives" (John 4:50). As the man was on his way home, his servants met him, saying that his son's fever was gone.

- When the disciples had fished all night and had caught nothing, He said, "Cast the net on the right side of the boat" (John 21:6). They did, and they took in an incredible catch of fish.

- To the paralytic in Capernaum, He said, "Arise, take up your bed, and go your way to your house" (Mark 2:11). He arose immediately and obeyed, amazing the crowd.

- When He healed the leper in Jerusalem, He said, "Show yourself to the priest" (Matt. 8:4).

- To the man born blind, the Lord commanded, "Go, wash in the pool of Siloam" (John 9:7). The man did as Jesus commanded and returned with his sight.

Many people say, "I will wait for the Lord to come to me." They don't realize that as believers we have the incredible ability to come into His throne room at any time. But we need to take the first step and say, "Lord, I need to hear Your voice."

When I am driving down the highway, the air is filled with radio signals. But I am only able to hear the sounds when I turn on my radio. And it is that way with God's voice. When we open the channels of communication, the Lord can begin to accomplish His purpose.

The First Word

I have learned through painful experiences that the first word I receive from the Lord is the one I must give. I can't second-guess God and turn to logic, intuition or the circumstances of the moment. With total faith and reliance on Him, I must give what comes to my heart.

When God speaks, He only needs to do it once. Scripture tells what happened to one prophet who was disobedient to God's first instructions.

During the reign of King Jeroboam in Israel, a prophet left Judah and went to Bethel as God had instructed him. While the king stood before the sacred altar burning incense, the prophet cried out,

> O altar, altar! Thus says the Lord: "Behold, a child, Josiah by name, shall be born to the house of David; and on you he shall sacrifice the priests of the high places who burn incense on you, and men's bones shall be burned on you"...This is the sign which the Lord has spoken: Surely the altar shall split apart, and the ashes on it shall be poured out (1 Kin. 13:2-3).

When King Jeroboam heard those words, he held out his

hand and said, "Arrest him!" And the hand that he stretched out toward the prophet withered so that he couldn't even draw it back toward his body (v. 4). Then, as was prophesied, the altar was split apart and the ashes were poured out.

Jeroboam immediately turned to the man of God and said, "Please entreat the favor of the Lord your God, and pray for me, that my hand may be restored to me" (v. 6). The prophet prayed, and the king's hand was completely healed. Then Jeroboam said, "Come home with me and refresh yourself, and I will give you a reward" (v. 7).

But God had told the prophet not to "eat bread, nor drink water, nor return by the same way you came" (v. 9). So he refused the king's offer and left the city by another route.

But that wasn't the end of the story. As the prophet was returning home, he was met by an older prophet, who asked him to come to his home to eat. The young prophet refused again, explaining what God had commanded him to do.

Then came the test. The older prophet said to him,

> I too am a prophet as you are, and an angel spoke to me by the word of the Lord, saying, "Bring him back with you to your house, that he may eat bread and drink water" (v. 18).

The old prophet was lying, but the young prophet believed him. So he went back with him, and they ate and drank together.

Then, as they sat at the table, the word of the Lord came to the old prophet, and he cried out:

> Thus says the Lord: "Because you have disobeyed the word of the Lord, and have not kept the commandment which the Lord your God com-

manded you...your corpse shall not come to the
tomb of your fathers" (vv. 21-22).

After the meal, the young man saddled his donkey and
continued his journey home. On the journey, "a lion met
him on the road and killed him" (v. 24). When the old
prophet heard what had happened, he said, "It is the man
of God who was disobedient to the word of the Lord," and
he mourned for him (v. 26).

When you hear the unmistakable voice of God, never
allow any man or woman — regardless of their credentials
— to lead you astray. Your future does not depend on the
alliance someone else has with God, but on *your* relationship with Him.

Don't "Shelve" It

The voice of the Lord is not an obscure, clouded impres-
sion, but a clear and distinct sound. If you think it sounds
good, but you are not sure it is God, then it probably *isn't*
the Lord. You need to be aware that many false prophets
can tell you many good things. But "good" is not always
God.

Some people listen to a prophetic word or a teaching
and say, "Well, if it is not from God, I will just file it. I'll put
it on the shelf." As believers we should not "shelve" anything. We should act immediately to either receive the voice
of God or reject a false message. Our decision should be
based on whether or not the word is confirmed in your
spirit.

False doctrine is simple to detect. You can turn to chapter and verse for a reference. But a prophet does not say,
"According to Scripture I am giving you this word." He
says, "Thus says the Lord," and you have to either accept it
or turn it away.

In some cases you may remain in a quandary regarding

the validity of a spoken word. Then you should pray earnestly for God's guidance. If you don't have peace in your heart, dismiss the message — regardless of whom the prophet is.

People who do not know how the Lord operates take a prophetic word and rush to presume what it means. Often they give their own interpretations, not God's. We need to slow down. If we hold on to what we receive, God will unfold it in His own time. Out of one revelation will spring another, then another, until the prophecy is fulfilled.

When you hear the voice of the Lord, you have only one obligation: to deliver it. But the prophet is often in a delicate position. If the people don't accept the word, they will chase him away. If he fails to speak the truth, God will punish him.

Those who become the voice of God are the watchmen of our day. But being a watchman carries with it a great burden. God told the prophet Ezekiel:

> Son of man, speak to the children of your people, and say to them: "When [the watchman] sees the sword coming upon the land, if he blows the trumpet and warns the people, then whoever hears the sound of the trumpet and does not take warning, if the sword comes and takes him away, his blood shall be on his own head" (Ezek. 33:2-4).

But what happens if the watchman sees danger coming and fails to blow the trumpet?

> [If] the sword comes and takes any person from among them, he is taken away in his iniquity; but his blood I will require at the watchman's hand (v. 6).

When God gives you a word — whatever the message — proclaim it loud and clear.

When Prophecy Fails

Some people seem surprised when I tell them, "Not everything a prophet says will happen." They have heard so many "name-it-and-claim-it" messages that they believe anything spoken by someone with a prophetic ministry will come to pass. But that is not always the case.

In these two specific instances, the voice of the Lord will not be fulfilled:

1. When people reject God's promise of hope and continue to live in their sins, God's word of blessing will not be fulfilled.

2. When people walk in disobedience to the *logos* (spoken) word and refuse to heed the commands of Christ.

Jonah was a chosen mouthpiece of God, but his prophecy did not come to pass. The Lord told him: "Arise, go to Nineveh, that great city, and cry out against it; for their wickedness has come up before Me" (Jon. 1:2).

The prophet fled from his mission and sailed for Tarshish. In the midst of a violent storm, he was thrown overboard and was swallowed by a great fish. Jonah repented and was thrown up on dry ground.

For the second time the voice of the Lord came and said, "Arise, go to Nineveh, that great city, and preach to it the message that I tell you." When he entered the city he cried out and said, "Yet forty days, and Nineveh shall be overthrown!" (Jon. 3:2,4).

But his prophecy did not happen. The people of Nineveh "believed God, proclaimed a fast, and put on sackcloth, from the greatest to the least of them" (v. 5).

The Lord saw that "they turned from their evil way; and God relented from the disaster that He had said He would bring upon them, and He did not do it" (v. 10). Ninevah's repentance canceled Jonah's prophetic word.

That scene is repeated many times in the Old Testament. God's spokesman pronounced havoc and calamity, but the people turned to the Lord and were spared.

At the cross, the prophet's message changed dramatically. The voice of the Lord became one of love, of hope and of promise. The word He now gives through His prophets — with few exceptions — is a bright and joyful sound.

The unmistakable difference between God's prophet and a false prophet is this: The Lord's spokesman only knows God's plan for your life; the fraudulent seer only knows the plan of Satan.

I become greatly concerned when people speak a word of destruction. For example, someone may make a great pronouncement such as, "There is going to be an earthquake on March 23." Ask yourself if that is an act of God or of Satan.

The Lord may know what the devil is going to do, but He certainly is not Satan's mouthpiece. Instead, the voice of the Lord is sent to reveal the plan of the Father for your life. He may show you where you are going wrong, but He will guide you to a path of safety. He prophesies *goodness*.

It is through God's voice that we can have a glimpse of the great things He has planned.

The Lord is still saying, "If you only knew!"

TEN

THE VOICE
OF HOPE

YOU HEAR it over and over — people who are perfectly healthy the day they retire are pronounced dead within two years.

Why does it happen? Because their future is gone. They have nothing to live for any longer.

When people talk about faith, hope and love (1 Cor. 13:13), they spend most of the time discussing faith and love. But they seem to forget what links them together — hope.

Prophets of God do not have a ministry of love, although they operate in love. They do not have a ministry of faith, although they operate by faith. Theirs is a ministry of hope — giving people something to live for.

One of the great proverbs says, "Where there is no vi-

THE SOUND OF HIS VOICE

sion, the people perish" (Prov. 29:18, KJV). In other words, knowing God's plan is essential to your life. I am often asked, "Why would the Lord want to tell me something that will happen twenty or thirty years from now?" I believe God reveals His plan for us so we may have confidence and security every day of our lives.

Sustaining Power

Scripture is filled with dramatic accounts of people whose lives had actually been extended so God's promises to them could be fulfilled.

God had a plan for Paul's life. He said Paul was "a chosen vessel of Mine to bear My name before Gentiles, kings, and the children of Israel" (Acts 9:15).

During his missionary journeys, Paul was repeatedly threatened with death, yet God miraculously kept him alive. Once, when the Jews in Jerusalem were plotting to kill Paul, the voice of the Lord came to him and said, "Be of good cheer, Paul; for as you have testified for Me in Jerusalem, so you must also bear witness at Rome" (Acts 23:11). In other words, your number isn't up yet!

The knowledge that he was going to witness in Rome sustained Paul in the face of great danger. Satan tried again and again to stop his journey. He was shipwrecked and placed in chains, but that did not discourage him. The voice of the Lord said there was something more he would accomplish.

Then it happened. Paul arrived in Rome and was placed under house arrest for two years — where he conveniently "received all who came to him, preaching the kingdom of God and teaching the things which concern the Lord Jesus Christ with all confidence, no one forbidding him" (Acts 28:31).

It makes no difference whether you are young or old. If you can catch the vision the Lord has for your life, He will keep you alive until you have completed the task.

Scripture tells us that "[King] David, after he nad served the purpose of God in his own generation, died, [and] was laid beside his ancestors" (Acts 13:36, NRSV).

You may say, "But I'm not like David or Paul. I don't have a great calling on my life." Never underestimate the voice of the Lord. God took you out of the womb, breathed His life into you and created a unique human being. He has raised you up for a purpose that no one else can accomplish.

A New Dimension

God will give you a glimpse of what lies far ahead if you are willing to enter a new spiritual dimension. That is what He did for the prophet Daniel. The Lord gave him a vision of things to come thousands of years into the future. God said:

> I have come to make you understand what will happen to your people in the latter days, for the vision refers to many days yet to come (Dan. 10:14).

However, God does not send prophets to be soothsayers. They do not come with a message that says, "Next year you are going to marry a person who has red hair" or "Sell your stock in IBM and buy Mobil Oil."

King David prayed, "Show me Your ways, O Lord; teach me Your paths" (Ps. 25:4). In this generation God is restoring the prophetic ministry to the church for the purpose of sharing the ways of God. I believe He wants us to understand His thoughts and what He is preparing for the days and years ahead. When the body of Christ understands what tomorrow holds, I believe they will move boldly forward in the power of the Spirit.

Inexpressible

Once God speaks to you, it is only the beginning of His divine communication. At first you may not recognize the Lord because His voice is not like yours and mine. He speaks in the realm of the spirit, and to spiritual "babes," those sounds may be unfamiliar.

But as you grow in grace, you are elevated to higher ground. The Lord draws closer, and the sounds become clear and distinct. His voice becomes the joy of your walk with Him.

At every act of obedience, God is communicating with you.

The Lord gives continual revelations to lead you from glory to glory as you achieve His plan for your life.

At times God may speak to you in words that are impossible to express. It may even take years to understand the meaning. Or what the Lord tells you may need to be held in confidence between you and God. The apostle Paul described how he was once "caught up into Paradise and heard inexpressible words, which it is not lawful for a man to utter" (2 Cor. 12:4).

Although the apostle received visions and revelations directly from God, he was not to boast about them. The Lord kept him humble by forcing him to deal with the problems of everyday life.

> And lest I should be exalted above measure by the abundance of the revelations, a thorn in the flesh was given to me, a messenger of Satan to buffet me, lest I be exalted above measure (v. 7).

God's plans and our emergencies often seem to be on different tracks, but the Lord knows exactly what we need. When the problems are the most severe, God proves Himself on behalf of individuals or nations.

Daniel was a man of faith and power, but he was thrown

into a den of savage lions — a place of shame, dishonor and danger. God's choice was to do something supernatural *there*. He closed the mouths of the lions, but he also addressed the root of the problem: the king's command to worship other gods. After Daniel survived the lions, the king made a decree that every person in the nation "must tremble and fear before the God of Daniel. For He is the living God, and steadfast forever; his kingdom is the one which shall not be destroyed, and His dominion shall endure to the end" (Dan. 6:26).

The same thing happened when Shadrach, Meshach and Abednego were thrown into the furnace of fire. It seemed as if their time on earth had ended. But in the hour of their greatest need, the Son of Man made an appearance on their behalf.

> King Nebuchadnezzar was astonished; and he rose in haste and spoke, saying to his counselors, "Did we not cast three men bound into the midst of the fire?"
>
> They answered and said to the king, "True, O king."
>
> "Look!" he answered, "I see four men loose, walking in the midst of the fire; and they are not hurt, and the form of the fourth is like the Son of God" (Dan. 3:24-25).

A Holy Habitation

One morning I told the Lord in prayer, "Lord, it seems as if Your church is being overwhelmed by the evils of Satan and by such an ungodly society."

Then I heard the voice of God saying, "Look in the Scriptures. I have only just begun. When the enemy seems to be prevailing against the kingdom, then I will make a judgment in favor of the saints."

171

The prophet Daniel said it long ago:

> I was watching; and the same horn was making
> war against the saints, and prevailing against
> them, until the Ancient of Days came, and a judg-
> ment was made in favor of the saints of the Most
> High, and the time came for the saints to possess
> the kingdom (Dan. 7:21-22).

Even though Satan seems to be coming against us, a time will come when the saints will prevail.

The Lord has shown me again and again that what is on the horizon is far greater than a breath of fresh air or a revival. And it is more than a visitation from above, in which the Lord comes, and then He leaves. We are going to experience a "habitation" of the Holy One. It will be permanent. He will come and reside!

The generation that God is raising up will cling to what the Lord provides. They will break down religious walls and say no to discord, contention and strife.

Just when God is about to do something great, Satan attempts to create havoc by attacking the children. I believe that the devil attempts to destroy a generation of children every time he realizes that God is about to unleash His awesome power. I believe he can sense it in the atmosphere.

When Christ was born, Satan knew that a chosen generation was just ahead and that the blood of the cross would redeem man for eternity. So what did Satan do? He planned an assault on innocent children.

When Herod heard that wise men had followed the star that heralded the birth of a holy child, he was

> exceedingly angry; and he sent forth and put to
> death all the male children who were in Bethle-
> hem and in all its districts, from two years old

and under, according to the time which he had determined from the wise men (Matt. 2:16).

But God prevailed, and the generation that launched the Christian church emerged.

Nearly two thousand years have passed, and Satan is in the midst of his third onslaught. He is spewing out his wrath on millions of children while they are in their mothers' wombs. This is the murder of abortion.

The devil knows that a generation is about to emerge that will usher in the King of kings. But God is speaking in these exciting times. For every child taken out by Satan, I believe the Lord will raise up two to praise His name.

Forever Strong

As we survey the battlefield, it may seem as if soldiers are falling, but the great conflict is just ahead. It is time for God's people to say, "Let God arise, let His enemies be scattered; let those also who hate Him flee before Him" (Ps. 68:1).

I am not waiting for God to judge a nation because of unrighteousness. Yes, the Bible says that what we sow, we will surely reap (Gal. 6:7). But it also tells us about a God whose mercy endures forever (Ps. 136:1ff.). I am waiting for God to pour out His great blessing on those who are honorable, righteous and cleansed by the blood of Christ.

How can we fulfill the purpose of God in our generation? The story of Caleb holds the answer. Caleb was a man who knew and understood God, but he was surrounded by pessimists and unbelievers. When Moses sent spies to check out the promised land, Caleb's report was:

"Let us go up at once and take possession, for we are well able to overcome it."
But the men who had gone up with him said,

"We are not able to go up against the people, for they are stronger than we" (Num. 13:30-31).

The people believed they were doomed to fail, so they refused to go into the promised land. You may say, "It's too bad that Caleb failed." But he didn't. Forty-five years later he was still serving God and was stronger than ever. At Gilgal, Caleb said to Joshua:

> I was forty years old when Moses the servant of the Lord sent me from Kadesh Barnea to spy out the land, and I brought back word to him as it was in my heart (Josh. 14:7).

He explained how others brought back a different report. Then he said, "but I wholly followed the Lord my God" (Josh. 14:8). And listen to this! Caleb said:

> Behold, the Lord has kept me alive, as He said, these forty-five years...and now, here I am this day, eighty-five years old. As yet I am as strong this day as I was on the day that Moses sent me; just as my strength was then, so now is my strength for war, both for going out and for coming in (vv. 10-11).

Caleb, even at that age, was ready to take on the giants. He said,

> Now therefore, give me this mountain of which the Lord spoke in that day; for you heard in that day how the Anakim [giants] were there...It may be that the Lord will be with me, and I shall be able to drive them out as the Lord said (v. 12).

How did Caleb retain the strength of his youth? He never,

ever turned his back on the voice of the Lord. As a result, God gave him a great inheritance (Josh 14:13).

You may feel that you are in a situation which makes it impossible to fulfill the promise of God. But don't give up. Keep His word alive, and the Lord will preserve you and allow you to see a stunning victory.

When Will It Happen?

I shudder to think what would have become of my life if I had never heard the voice of God. His messenger came to me when I was bleeding and dying in a filthy gutter outside that rock-and-roll club in Port Elizabeth.

But with my salvation He gave me a promise that has sustained me. No matter where I travel, I can still hear the words God spoke when Pastor Pretorious lifted me out of the waters of baptism. The Lord not only called me to the ministry, but He said, "None of your household will go to the grave without salvation."

When my parents resisted me because of the radical turn-around I experienced, I wondered, *How can it happen? How can they ever be saved?* The tension in our home felt like a wire that had been stretched to the breaking point.

But God began to give me signs of encouragement. A few months after my conversion, my sister, Shelley, saw that the transformation in my life was genuine. She asked questions about Jesus and finally gave her heart to the Lord. She began attending church with me.

Day after day I prayed that a miracle would happen in the lives of my parents. But there was no response. All I could cling to was the promise I heard God speak.

While I served my "apostolic apprenticeship" as a new convert, and when I was on duty in the South African army, I was increasingly concerned for my mother. She had become crippled with arthritis. It broke my heart to see her in pain, with stiffness, swelling and inflammation of the joints.

One day when I was on the staff of the Pentecostal Protestant Church in Port Elizabeth, I said to my mother, "Why don't you come to church with me tonight?" An older evangelist, Reverend Arthur Nipper, was conducting special services.

I was surprised when both my mother *and* my father came with me. The power of God was so strong during that meeting that I was expecting a miracle to take place in their lives. But they left the building with no response.

Later that night I was thrilled when Mom took me aside and said, "Kim, do you think you could have that minister come and pray for me?"

"Of course," I assured her.

The next day evangelist Nipper drove to our home and anointed my mother with oil and prayed for her healing.

"Something is happening," she said. The swelling in her body began to subside. "The pain is gone!" she exclaimed.

Instantly, my mother was healed — and she had not even received salvation yet! Several days later, while she was thanking God for her miracle, she prayed the sinner's prayer and asked that the blood of Christ would cleanse her from her sin.

But that's not all. In the middle of the night, while she was reading the book of Acts, she received the baptism of the Holy Spirit just as it was recorded at Pentecost.

My father was another story. He was still a skeptic. It seemed that nothing we could say or do would bring him into the kingdom. "But, Lord, You promised!" I kept praying even after I moved to Durban, was married and began traveling in ministry.

Then came that devastating moment in 1986 at the air terminal in Canada. My family was with me, and we were about to pick up tickets to fly to a meeting in the United States. I'll never forget the concerned look on the woman's face at the counter when she asked, "Are you Mr. Clement?"

"Yes, I am," I replied. "Is there some kind of a problem?"

"I have been asked to give you this message. Your father has died in South Africa."

Instantly, I became nauseated, and tears rushed to my eyes. But in that moment the Lord said again, "Do you remember My word?" Of course I did. Years before, God had promised, "None of your household will go to the grave without salvation."

The clerk looked puzzled when I told her, "It's impossible! The Lord told me he is not going to die. He's not saved yet."

"Well, I don't know anything about that," she said, "but this is the message I was told to give you. I'm very sorry."

It is difficult to explain, but when God reminded me of His voice, He also gave me a peace and serenity that was beyond description.

When I reached my mother by phone in Uitenhage, she was obviously upset.

"Tell me what has happened to Daddy," I said. "I was told that he died."

"No," she said. "We told them to tell you that he is *dying*. The doctors have given him only a few hours to live." I learned that my father had suffered a massive stroke and was in a coma, totally paralyzed. "They are telling me that he will never walk or talk again," she said.

At that moment, God gave me a special word which I tried to tell her, but she kept interrupting. "Kim, they told me he's not going to make it. It is the most severe type of stroke anyone can have."

Through her tears I said, "Mom, listen to me! Don't talk like that. He is going to make it because I had a word from God."

She calmed down long enough for me to tell her, "God said that He's going to live and not die. He's going to walk, talk and be normal."

I repeated what God said, but I'm not sure she understood.

I was so sure of what the Lord told me that I did not cancel my speaking schedule. Instead I continued my ministry and kept in touch with my mother by phone.

After several weeks in a coma, my father suddenly opened his eyes. He began to speak. He began to move his legs and arms. My mother called and said, "Kim, your father asked me to pray with him. He asked Jesus to come into his heart!" That was one of the happiest moments of my life. God's words to me had been fulfilled.

Later I flew back to South Africa to visit him. It was difficult to see him in a wheelchair, but God was doing a great work of healing. He called me to his room and said, "Kim, I want everything God has for me. I would like to be filled with the Spirit. Will you pray with me?"

We had a revival right there! Not only did he receive the Pentecostal experience, but the glory of God swept over both of us. For years my father and I had nothing in common at all. Now there was an incredible connection bonding us together.

Not only was he saved and filled with the Spirit, but God has extended his life. As I write these words, he is still fully recovered, able to walk and thanking God for His unspeakable gift.

Death Was Defied

I will never fully understand the mysteries of how God works. My older brother, Barry, was diagnosed with Hodgkin's disease, a type of cancer that affects the lymph nodes. Like my father, he was given only a short time to live. He refused God until the very end.

As his condition was deteriorating, the Lord allowed me to be at his side. Again, I prayed, "Lord, You told me they would all be saved!"

I was able to pray with Barry as he called on Jesus. Two months later I had the joy of baptizing him in water. He was also healed totally of his cancer. To me, there is no question that death was defied because of the voice of God.

My younger brother, David, was the last in our family to be touched by the power of God. He accepted Christ in 1992.

I wish I could tell you that when you hear the voice of God, everything will suddenly be perfect. Members of my family continue to struggle with the issues of life because Satan still stalks the earth. There is one thing, however, on which we can depend. God said, "My word...shall not return to Me void, but it shall accomplish what I please, and it shall prosper in the thing for which I sent it" (Is. 55:11).

> It is my prayer that you will *receive* the voice of
> God.
> I pray that you will *believe* the voice of God.
> Start today to act upon it in faith.
> And I pray that you will *become* the voice of
> God to those who need the Savior.

If you enjoyed *The Sound of His Voice*, you'll love
these other new Creation House titles:

Hippo in the Garden
by James Ryle
Author James Ryle says that God speaks to us at
unusual times in unexpected places. Through his
humorous personal anecdotes and references to
the Old and New Testament Scriptures, you will
discover that every circumstance of life becomes
an opportunity to converse with God.

Passion for Jesus
by Mike Bickle
The Song of Solomon, a prophetic song describing
the church's awakening of passionate love for God
and the maturing of her fervent devotion,
is the focus of Mike Bickle's new book,
Passion for Jesus. This contagious message
will bring you into a new and exciting life
and help you gain an extravagant love for God.

Final Approach
by Roberts Liardon
Sometimes Christians get so caught up in debates
about the end times that they forget the real purpose
for being here on earth. That's the foundational truth
behind Roberts Liardon's latest release,
Final Approach. It offers readers a refreshing,
positive guide to living in the end times.

Available at your local Christian bookstore or from:

Creation House
600 Rinehart Road
Lake Mary, FL 32746
1-800-451-4598